Abbie,

You always tell me how greatful you are to know me, and you should be! (3/c)

No, actually it's me who has been with knowing you. It's like God

human angel, and you are one of mi

This wasn't the original book that I wanted to get you, but I hope you enjoy it as much as I do.

I want to thank you for being a sister to me this year, I know that we've had a rough time together, but I have a feeling God has so much more planned for us in the future.

Happy Birthday

Love in Christ,

Karen

The Lamb's Supper

SCOTT HAHN

The Lamb's Supper

The Mass as Heaven on Earth

DOUBLEDAY

New York London Toronto Sydney Auckland

PUBLISHED BY DOUBLEDAY
a division of Random House, Inc.
1540 Broadway, New York, New York 10036

DOUBLEDAY and the portrayal of an anchor with a dolphin are trademarks of
Doubleday, a division of Random House, Inc.

Library of Congress Cataloging-in-Publication Data
Hahn, Scott.
The lamb's supper: the Mass as heaven on Earth / by Scott Hahn.
—1st ed.
p.   cm.
1. Mass—Celebration.   2. Bible. N.T. Revelation—Criticism,
interpretation, etc.   I. Title.
BX2230.5.H29   1999
264'.02036—dc21   99-23679
CIP

Nihil Obstat: Rev. James Dunfee, Censor Librorum
Imprimatur: ✠ Most Rev. Gilbert Sheldon, Bishop of Steubenville

The *Nihil Obstat* and *Imprimatur* are official declarations that a book or
pamphlet is free of doctrinal or moral error. No implication is contained
therein that those who have granted the *Nihil Obstat* and *Imprimatur* agree
with the contents, opinions, or statements expressed.

To Kimberly

Contents

Contents

Contents

Foreword

Fr. Benedict J. Groeschel C.F.R.

T HIS REMARKABLE BOOK brings together several powerful spiritual realities—all of them important to the believing Christian, and all of them apparently so diverse as to superficially appear unrelated: the end of the world and the daily Mass; the Apocalypse and the Lord's Supper; the humdrum of daily life and the *Parousia,* the coming of the Lord.

If you are a cradle Catholic like myself, Dr. Hahn is likely to leave you with a whole new appreciation of the Mass. If you entered the Church or are thinking of coming into full communion with it, then he will show you a dimension of Catholic Christianity that you probably never thought about—its eschatology, or teaching on the end of time. In fact, relatively few Catholics realize the link between the celebration of the Eucharist and the end of the world.

The salient feature of *The Lamb's Supper* is its moving and lucid appreciation of the reality of the Liturgy of the Eucharist, the act of worship given to us by our High Priest on the eve of His sacrificial death. Dr. Hahn explores this mysterious reality with all the zeal and enthusiasm of a new convert.

I can only contrast this with my own experience—this year I will celebrate (quietly) my fifty-seventh anniversary as an altar boy. Yet when Scott called me and asked me somewhat cautiously to write a foreword to his new book, based on the very ancient eschatological interpretation of the Eucharist given by the Eastern Fathers of the second to the sixth centuries, I responded with "Well, of course, this is what I thought about the Eucharist for decades."

The Mass, or, as it's more accurately called in the Eastern Churches, the Divine Liturgy, is so rich a reality that there are as many valid theological approaches to it as there are to the whole mystery of Christ Himself. The Eucharist is part of the great living mountain which is Christ, a simile drawn from the ancient saints of the Holy Land. This mountain can be approached from many sides. This eschatological approach is one of the most intriguing and fruitful.

I always feel a twinge of annoyance when I see in a college or a hotel a list of "religious services" and observe the Mass listed at 9 A.M. The Mass is not a religious service. When Catholics say morning prayer or the recitation of the rosary or even have Benediction of the Blessed Sacrament, that's a service. It's something that we do for God, similar to the public prayer of any religious denomination. But the Holy Sacrifice of the Eucharist, the Divine Liturgy, is not precisely—in its essence—done by man at all.

Let me tell you, I've been a priest for forty years and I never conducted a "service" called a Mass. I was a "stand-in" for the High Priest, to use the words of Church teaching, I was there functioning *in persona Christi*—in the person of Christ, the High Priest of the Epistle to the Hebrews. People do not come to Mass to receive my body and blood, and I could not have given it to them if they did. They come for communion with Christ.

This is the mysterious element in all Christian sacraments—including baptism. For this reason, in case of great necessity anyone can function *in persona Christi* to give baptism, because it is Christ who actually baptizes. It is Christ who forgives sin, Christ who prepares thy dying, Christ who ordains and who blesses the marriages.

Like Catholic and Orthodox Christians who think about it (as well as some Anglicans and even some Lutherans), I believe that Christ is the Priest of all the sacraments, just as He speaks to us from every page of Sacred Scripture. He ministers to us in every sacrament— and we experience in this way the vitality of His mystical body.

When you read Dr. Hahn's account of the Eucharist as the heavenly worship spoken of in Revelation, as he indicates so well, you should begin to tingle with the vitality of grace.

The Mass on earth is the presentation of the marriage supper of the Lamb. As Dr. Hahn points out, most

Christians either sidestep the Book of Revelation and its mysterious signs or they spin their own peculiar little theories about who is who and where it's all going to end. As an inhabitant of New York City (the twentieth-century candidate for Babylon), I'm perfectly delighted with the prospect of it all ending soon, even next week. But I am tired of all these prophets of doom and their interpretations. Promises, promises! Early in this century, I lived through the careers of several guys who were on the short list of candidates for the big antichrist, and no show.

My love for Revelation is not based on all this Star Wars paranoia, but on the wonderful view of the heavenly Jerusalem in the final chapters of Revelation. These come as close as you can to describing what eye has not seen nor ear heard. Now with the reading and rereading of *The Lamb's Supper,* many other chapters are open to me much more clearly—describing in symbolic form what the eternal life of the saints may be like, to use St. Augustine's phrase.

It was St. Augustine, you know, who insisted on putting Revelation as well as Hebrews in the New Testament Canon at an African bishops' council held at the end of the fourth century. Again, to quote Augustine, we may in prayer by His great mercy "touch for an instant that Fountain of Life where He feeds Israel forever." But apart from these special moments of contemplation, we may see symbolically at the daily celebration of Mass the realities of the heavenly worship of the High Priest and His mystical body.

I am grateful to Dr. Hahn for finding and bringing back to life this vision of the early Fathers of the Church.

The only thing that we ever do in this world that is real participation in the life we hope to live forever is to worship with Christ at the Liturgy. However humble the appointments of the church buildings, however limited the spiritual insight of the participants, when we are at the Liturgy of the Mass, Christ is there and mysteriously we are for that moment standing at the Eternal Supper of the Lamb. Read carefully this book, and you will learn how and why.

"Behold, I stand at the door and knock; if anyone hears My voice and opens the door, I will come in to him and eat with him, and he with Me . . . After this I looked, and lo, in heaven an open door . . ." —Revelation 3:20, 4:1

PART ONE

The Gift
of the Mass

INTRODUCTION

Christ Stands at the Door

THE MASS REVEALED

O F ALL THINGS CATHOLIC, there is nothing so familiar as the Mass. With its timeless prayers, hymns, and gestures, the Mass is like home to us. Yet most Catholics will go a lifetime without seeing beyond the surface of memorized prayers. Few will glimpse the *powerful supernatural drama* they enter into every Sunday. Pope John Paul II has called the Mass "heaven on earth," explaining that "the liturgy we celebrate on earth is a mysterious participation in the heavenly liturgy."

The Mass is near and dear. The Book of Revelation, on the other hand, seems remote and puzzling. Page after page flashes bizarre and frightening images: of wars and plagues, beasts and angels, rivers of blood, demonic frogs, and seven-headed dragons. And the most sympathetic character is a seven-horned, seven-eyed lamb. "If that's just the surface," some Catholics say, "I don't think I want to see the depths."

Well, in this little book, I'd like to propose something outlandish. I propose that the key to understanding the Mass is the biblical Book of Revelation—and, further, that the Mass is the only way a Christian can truly make sense of the Book of Revelation.

If you're skeptical, you should know that you're not alone. When I told a friend that I was writing about the Mass as a key to the Book of Revelation, she laughed and said, "Revelation? Isn't that just weird stuff?"

It does seem weird to Catholics, because, for many years, we have been reading the book apart from Christian tradition. The interpretations most people know today are the ones that have made the news or the bestseller charts, and those have been overwhelmingly Protestant. I know this from my own experience. I've been studying the Book of Revelation for more than twenty years. Until 1985 I studied it as a Protestant minister, and, down through those years, I found myself engaged, in turn, by most of the fashionable and unfashionable interpretive theories. I tried every key, but none could open the door. Every now and then, I heard a tumbler click, and that gave me hope. Yet only when I began to contemplate the Mass did I feel the door begin to give way, a little bit at a time. Gradually, I found myself taken up by the great Christian tradition, and in 1986 I was received into full communion with the Catholic Church. After that, in my study of the Book of Revelation, matters became clearer. "After this I looked, and lo, in heaven an open door!" (Rev 4:1). And the door opened onto . . . Sunday Mass in your parish church.

Now, you may reply that your weekly experience of Mass is anything but heavenly. In fact, it's an uncomfortable hour, punctuated by babies screaming, bland hymns sung off-key, meandering, pointless homilies, and neighbors dressed as if they were going to a ball game, the beach, or a picnic.

Yet I insist that we *do* go to heaven when we go to Mass, and this is true of *every* Mass we attend, regardless of the quality of the music or the fervor of the preaching. This is not a matter of learning to "look at the bright side" of sloppy liturgies. This is not about developing a more charitable attitude toward tone-deaf cantors. This is all about something that's objectively true, something as real as the heart that beats within you. The Mass—and I mean *every* single Mass—is heaven on earth.

I assure you that this is not my idea; it is the Church's. Neither is it a new idea; it's been around since the day John had his apocalyptic vision. Yet it's an idea that hasn't caught on with Catholics in recent centuries— and I can't figure out why. Most of us will admit that we want to "get more" out of the Mass. Well, we can't get any more than heaven itself.

I should say from the start that this book is not a "Bible study." It is focused on the practical application of just one aspect of the Book of Revelation, and our study is far from exhaustive. Scholars debate endlessly about who wrote the Book of Revelation, and when, and where, and why, and on what sort of parchment. In this book, I will not take up these questions in any great detail. Neither have I written a handbook on the rubrics of the liturgy. Revelation is a mystical book, not a training video or a how-to manual.

Throughout this book, you will probably encounter the Mass in new ways—ways other than the one you're used to attending. Though heaven touches down whenever the Church celebrates the Eucharist, the Mass looks different from place to place and time to time. Where I live, most Catholics are accustomed to the liturgy of the Latin Rite. (In fact, the word "Mass" properly refers *only* to the Eucharistic liturgy of the Latin Rite.) But there are many Eucharistic liturgies in the Catholic Church: the Ambrosian, Armenian, Byzantine, Chaldean, Coptic, Malabar, Malankar, Maronite, Melkite, and Ruthenian, among others. Each has its own beauty; each has its own wisdom; each shows us a different corner of heaven on earth.

Researching *The Lamb's Supper* has given me new eyes to see the Mass. I pray that reading this book gives the same gift to you. Together, let's ask for a new heart as well, so that, through our study and prayer, we may grow more and more to love the Christian mysteries that we have from the Father.

The Book of Revelation will show us the Mass as *heaven on earth*. Now, let's press on, without delay, because heaven can't wait.

ONE

In Heaven Right Now

WHAT I FOUND
AT MY FIRST MASS

THERE I STOOD, a man incognito, a Protestant minister in plainclothes, slipping into the back of a Catholic chapel in Milwaukee to witness my first Mass. Curiosity had driven me there, and I still didn't feel sure that it was *healthy* curiosity. Studying the writings of the earliest Christians, I'd found countless references to "the liturgy," "the Eucharist," "the sacrifice." For those first Christians, the Bible—the book I loved above all—was incomprehensible apart from the event that today's Catholics called "the Mass."

I wanted to understand the early Christians; yet I'd had no experience of liturgy. So I persuaded myself to go and see, as a sort of academic exercise, but vowing all along that I would neither kneel nor take part in idolatry.

I took my seat in the shadows, in a pew at the very back of that basement chapel. Before me were a goodly number of worshipers, men and women of all ages. Their genuflections impressed me, as did their apparent concentration in prayer. Then a bell rang, and they all stood as the priest emerged from a door beside the altar.

Unsure of myself, I remained seated. For years, as an evangelical Calvinist, I'd been trained to believe that the Mass was the ultimate sacrilege a human could commit. The Mass, I had been taught, was a ritual that purported to "resacrifice Jesus Christ." So I would remain an observer. I would stay seated, with my Bible open beside me.

SOAKED IN SCRIPTURE

As the Mass moved on, however, something hit me. My Bible wasn't just beside me. It was before me—*in the words of the Mass!* One line was from Isaiah, another from the Psalms, another from Paul. The experience was overwhelming. I wanted to stop everything and shout, "Hey, can I explain what's happening from Scripture? This is great!" Still, I maintained my observer status. I remained on the sidelines until I heard the priest pronounce the words of consecration: "This is My body . . . This is the cup of My blood."

Then I felt all my doubt drain away. As I saw the priest raise that white host, I felt a prayer surge from my heart in a whisper: *"My Lord and my God. That's really you!"*

I was what you might call a basket case from that point. I couldn't imagine a greater excitement than what those words had worked upon me. Yet the experience was intensified just a moment later, when I heard the congregation recite: "Lamb of God . . . Lamb of God . . .

Lamb of God," and the priest respond, *"This* is the Lamb of God . . ." as he raised the host.

In less than a minute, the phrase "Lamb of God" had rung out four times. From long years of studying the Bible, I immediately knew where I was. I was in the Book of Revelation, where Jesus is called the Lamb no less than twenty-eight times in twenty-two chapters. I was at the marriage feast that John describes at the end of that very last book of the Bible. I was before the throne of heaven, where Jesus is hailed forever as the Lamb. I wasn't ready for this, though—I was at Mass!

HOLY SMOKE!

I would return to Mass the next day, and the next day, and the next. Each time I went back, I would "discover" more of the Scriptures fulfilled before my eyes. Yet no book was as visible to me, in that dark chapel, as the Book of Revelation, the Apocalypse, which describes the worship of the angels and saints in heaven. As in that book, so in that chapel, I saw robed priests, an altar, a congregation chanting "holy, holy, holy." I saw the smoke of incense; I heard the invocation of angels and saints; I myself sang the alleluias, for I was drawn ever more into this worship. I continued to sit in the back pew with my Bible, and I hardly knew which way to turn—toward the action in the Apocalypse or the action at the altar. More and more, they seemed to be the very same action.

I plunged with renewed vigor into my study of ancient Christianity and found that the earliest bishops, the Fathers of the Church, had made the same "discovery" I was making every morning. They considered the Book of Revelation the key to the liturgy, and the liturgy the key to the Book of Revelation. Something powerful was happening to me as a scholar and a believer. The book of the Bible that I had found most perplexing—the Book of Revelation—was now illuminating the ideas that were most foundational to my faith: the idea of the covenant as the sacred bond of the family of God. Moreover, the action that I had considered the supreme blasphemy—the Mass—now turned out to be the event that sealed God's covenant. "This is the cup of My blood, the blood of the new and everlasting covenant."

I was giddy with the newness of it all. For years I had been trying to make sense of the Book of Revelation as some kind of encoded message about the end of the world, about worship in faraway heaven, about something most Christians couldn't experience while still on earth. Now, after two weeks of daily Mass attendance, I found myself wanting to stand up during the liturgy and say, "Hey, everybody. Let me show you where you are in the Apocalypse! Turn to chapter four, verse eight. You're in heaven right now."

STEALING MY THUNDER

In heaven right now! The Fathers of the Church showed me that this wasn't *my* discovery. They had preached about it more than a thousand years ago. I was, however, convinced I deserved credit for the *rediscovery* of the relationship between the Mass and the Book of Revelation. Then I discovered that the Second Vatican Council had stolen my thunder. Consider the following words from the Constitution on the Sacred Liturgy:

> In the earthly liturgy we share in a foretaste of that heavenly liturgy which is celebrated in the Holy City of Jerusalem toward which we journey as pilgrims, where Christ is sitting at the right hand of God, Minister of the sanctuary and of the true tabernacle. With all the warriors of the heavenly army we sing a hymn of glory to the Lord; venerating the memory of the saints, we hope for some part and fellowship with them; we eagerly await the Savior, our Lord Jesus Christ, until He, our life, shall appear and we too will appear with Him in glory.

Wait a minute. That's heaven. No, it's the Mass. No, it's the Book of Revelation. Wait a minute: it's all of the above.

I found myself trying hard to go slowly, cautiously, careful to avoid the dangers to which converts are susceptible; for I was fast becoming a convert to the Catholic faith. Yet this discovery was not the product of an overwrought imagination; it was the solemn teaching of a council of the Catholic Church. In time, I would discover that it was also the inevitable conclusion of the most rigorous and honest Protestant scholars. One of them, Leonard Thompson, has written that "Even a cursory reading of the Book of Revelation shows the presence of liturgical language set in worship. . . . [T]he language of worship plays an important role in unifying the book." The images of liturgy alone can make that strange book make sense. Liturgical figures are central to its message,

Thompson writes, revealing "something more than visions of 'things to come.' "

COMING ATTRACTIONS

The Book of Revelation was about *Someone* Who was to come. It was about Jesus Christ and His "Second Coming," which is the way Christians have commonly translated the Greek word *Parousia*. Through hour after hour in that chapel in Milwaukee in 1985, I came to know that that Someone was the same Jesus Christ Whom the Catholic priest lifted up in the host. If the early Christians were correct, I knew that, in that very moment, heaven touched down on earth. *"My Lord and my God. That's really You!"*

Still, serious questions remained in my mind and heart—about the nature of sacrifice, about the biblical foundations of the Mass, about the continuity of Catholic tradition, about many of the small details of liturgical worship. These questions would define my investigations through the months leading up to my reception into the Catholic Church. In a sense, they continue to define my work today. These days, however, I ask not as an accuser or a curiosity seeker, but as a son who approaches his father, asking the impossible, asking to hold a bright and distant star in the palm of his hand.

I don't believe Our Father will refuse me, or you, the wisdom we seek regarding His Mass. It is, after all, the event in which He seals His covenant with us and makes us His children. This book is more or less a record of what I have found while investigating the riches of our

Catholic tradition. Our heritage includes the whole of the Bible, the uninterrupted witness of the Mass, the constant teachings of the saints, the research of the schools, the methods of contemplative prayer, and the pastoral care of the popes and bishops. In the Mass, you and I have heaven on earth. The evidence is overwhelming. The experience is a revelation.

TWO

Given for You

THE STORY OF SACRIFICE

THE PHRASE in the Mass that knocked me out was the "Lamb of God," because I knew that this Lamb was Jesus Christ Himself.

No one has to tell you that. Perhaps you've sung or recited the words a thousand times: "Lamb of God, You take away the sins of the world, have mercy on us." Just as many times you've seen the priest elevate the broken Host and proclaim, "This is the Lamb of God . . ." The Lamb is Jesus. This is not news; it's the kind of fact we gloss over. Jesus is many things, after all: He is Lord, God, Savior, Messiah, King, Priest, Prophet . . . and Lamb.

Yet, if we were really thinking, we wouldn't gloss over that last title. Look again at that list: Lord, God, Savior, Messiah, King, Priest, Prophet—and Lamb. One of these things is not like the others. The first seven are titles with which we could comfortably address a God-Man. They're titles with dignity, implying wisdom, power, and social status. But Lamb? Again, I ask you to divest yourself of two thousand years of accumulated symbolic meaning. Pretend for a moment that you've never sung the "Lamb of God."

ON THE LAMB

The title, then, seems almost comical in its inappropriateness. Lambs don't usually rank high on lists of most-admired animals. They're not particularly strong, clever, quick, or handsome. Other animals would seem more worthy. We can easily imagine Jesus, for example, as the Lion of Judah (Rev 5:5). Lions are kingly; they're strong and agile; nobody messes with the king of beasts. But the Lion of Judah makes only a cameo appearance in the Book of Revelation. Meanwhile, the Lamb dominates, appearing no less than twenty-eight times. The Lamb rules, occupying heaven's throne (Rev 22:3). It is the Lamb Who leads an army of hundreds of thousands of men and angels, striking fear in the hearts of the wicked (Rev 6:15–16). This last image, of the fierce and frightening Lamb, is almost too incongruous to imagine with a straight face.

Yet, for John, this matter of the Lamb is serious. The titles "Lamb" and "Lamb of God" are applied to Jesus almost exclusively in the books of the New Testament that are attributed to John: the Fourth Gospel and the Book of Revelation. Though other New Testament books (see

Acts 8:32–35; 1 Pet 1:19) say that Jesus is *like* a lamb in certain respects, only John dares to *call* Jesus "the Lamb" (see Jn 1:36 and throughout the Apocalypse).

We know that the Lamb is central to both the Mass and the Book of Revelation. And we know *Who* the Lamb is. However, if we want to experience the Mass as heaven on earth, we need to know more. We need to know *what* the Lamb is, and *why* we call Him "Lamb." To find out, we have to go back in time, almost to the very beginning.

WELL BREAD

To ancient Israel, the lamb was identified with sacrifice, and sacrifice is one of the most primal forms of worship. As early as the second generation described in Genesis, we find, in the story of Cain and Abel, the first recorded example of a sacrificial offering. "Cain brought to the Lord an offering of the fruit of the ground, and Abel brought of the firstlings of his flock and of their fat portions" (Gen 4:3–4). In due time, we encounter similar burnt offerings from Noah (Gen 8:20–21), Abraham (Gen 15:8–10; 22:13), Jacob (Gen 46:1), and others. In Genesis, the patriarchs were forever building altars, and altars served primarily as places of sacrifice. In addition to burnt offerings, the ancients sometimes poured "libations," or sacrificial offerings of wine.

Of the sacrifices in Genesis, two deserve our most careful attention: that of Melchizedek (Gen 14:18–20) and that of Abraham and Isaac in Genesis 22.

Melchizedek appears as the first priest mentioned in the Bible, and many Christians (following the Letter to the Hebrews 7:1–17) have seen him as a foreshadowing of Jesus Christ. Melchizedek was both priest and king, an odd combination in the Old Testament, but one that would later be applied to Jesus. Genesis describes Melchizedek as king of Salem, a land that would later become "Jeru-salem," meaning "City of Peace" (see Ps 76:2). Jesus would arise one day as king of the heavenly Jerusalem and, again like Melchizedek, "Prince of Peace." Finally, Melchizedek's sacrifice was extraordinary in that it involved no animals. He offered bread and wine, as Jesus would at the Last Supper, when He instituted the Eucharist. Melchizedek's sacrifice ended with a blessing upon Abraham.

MORIAH CARRY

Abraham himself would revisit the site of Salem, some years later, when God called upon him to make an ultimate sacrifice. In Genesis 22, God tells Abraham: "Take your son, your only son Isaac, whom you love, and go to the land of Moriah, and offer him there as a burnt offering upon one of the mountains" (v. 2). Israelite tradition, recorded in the 2 Chronicles 3:1, identifies Moriah with the future Temple site in Jerusalem. There Abraham traveled with Isaac, who carried upon his back the wood for the sacrifice (Gen 22:6). When Isaac asked where was the victim, Abraham replied, "God will provide Himself the lamb for a burnt offering, my son" (v. 8). In the end, the angel of God did stay Abraham's hand from sacrificing his son and provided a ram to be sacrificed.

In this story, Israel would discern God's covenant

oath to make Abraham's descendants a mighty nation: "By myself I have sworn . . . because you . . . have not withheld your son . . . I will multiply your descendants as the stars of heaven . . . and by your descendants shall all the nations of the earth bless themselves" (Gen 22:16–17). That was God's IOU to Abraham; it would also turn out to be Israel's life-insurance policy. In the desert of Sinai, when the chosen people earned death by worshiping the golden calf, Moses invoked God's covenant oath to Abraham in order to save them from divine wrath (see Ex 32:13–14).

Christians would later look upon the story of Abraham and Isaac as a profound allegory for the sacrifice of Jesus upon the cross. The similarities were many. First, Jesus, like Isaac, was a faithful father's only beloved son. Again like Isaac, Jesus carried uphill the wood for His own sacrifice, which would be consummated on a hill in Jerusalem. In fact, the site where Jesus died, Calvary, was one of the hillocks on Moriah's range. Moreover, the very first line of the New Testament identifies Jesus with Isaac as "the son of Abraham" (Mt 1:1). To Christian readers, even Abraham's words proved prophetic. Recall that there was no punctuation in the Hebrew original, and consider an alternate reading of verse 8: "God will provide Himself, the Lamb, for a burnt offering." The Lamb foreshadowed, of course, was Jesus Christ, God Himself— "that in Christ Jesus the blessing of Abraham might come upon the gentiles" (Gal 3:14; see also Gn 22:16–18).

ANIMAL MAGNETISM

By the time of Israel's enslavement in Egypt, it is clear that sacrifice occupies an essential and central part of Israel's religion. Pharaoh's overseers taunt that the Israelites' frequent sacrifices are merely an excuse for avoiding work (see Ex 5:17). Later, when Moses makes his appeal to Pharaoh, chief among his demands is the Israelites' right to offer sacrifice to God (see Ex 10:25).

What did all these offerings mean? Animal sacrifice meant many things to the ancient Israelites.

- It was a recognition of God's sovereignty over creation: "The earth is the Lord's" (Ps 24:1). Man acknowledged this fact by giving back to God what is ultimately His. Thus, sacrifice praised God from Whom all blessings flow.
- A sacrifice could be an act of thanks. Creation is given to man as a gift, but what return can man make to God (see Ps 116:12)? We can only give back what we ourselves have received.
- Sometimes, sacrifice served as a way of solemnly sealing an agreement or oath, a covenant before God (see Gen 21:22–32).
- Sacrifice could also be an act of renunciation and sorrow for sins. The person offering sacrifice recognized that his sins deserved death; he offered the animal's life in place of his own.

COUNTING SHEEP

But the pivotal sacrifice in Israel's history was the Passover, which precipitated the Israelites' flight from Egypt. It was at the Passover that God instructed each Israelite family to take an unblemished lamb without broken bones, kill it, and sprinkle its blood on the doorpost. That night, the Israelites were to eat the lamb. If they did, their firstborn would be spared. If they didn't, their firstborn would die in the night, along with all the firstborn in their flocks (see Ex 12:1–23). The sacrificial lamb died as a ransom, in place of the firstborn of the household. The Passover, then, was an act of redemption, a "buying back."

Yet God did not merely *rescue* the firstborn sons of Israel; He also consecrated them as a "kingdom of priests, a holy nation" (Ex 19:6)—a nation He called His own "firstborn son" (Ex 4:22).

The Lord told the Israelites, then, to commemorate the Passover every year, and He even gave them the words they should use to explain the ritual to future generations: "When your children say to you, 'What do you mean by this service?' you shall say, 'It is the sacrifice of the Lord's Passover, for He passed over the houses of the people of Israel in Egypt, when He slew the Egyptians'" (Ex 12:26–27).

Entering the Promised Land, the Israelites continued their daily sacrifices to God, now guided by the many prescriptions of the Law, which we see enumerated in

Leviticus, Numbers, and Deuteronomy. (See, for example, Lev 7–9; Num 28; Dt 16.)

ALTARED STATE: JERUSALEM AS ROYAL CAPITAL

With the establishment of the Temple at Jerusalem around 960 B.C., Israel offered its daily sacrifices to Almighty God in a majestic setting. Each day, the priests sacrificed two lambs, one in the morning and one in the evening, to atone for the sins of the nation. Those were the essential sacrifices; but, throughout the day, the smoke rose from many other, private offerings. Goats, bulls, turtledoves, pigeons, and rams were offered on the huge bronze altar that stood in the open air at the entrance to the inner court of the Temple. The "Holy Place" of the Temple was just beyond that altar, and the "Holy of Holies"—the dwelling place of God—was farther still. The "altar of incense" stood immediately before the Holy of Holies. Only priests were permitted into the inner court of the Temple; only the high priest was permitted in the Holy of Holies, and even he could enter only briefly, and only once a year, on the Day of Atonement, Yom Kippur. For even the high priest was a sinner and thus unworthy to abide in God's presence.

The Jerusalem Temple brought together all the strains of sacrifice that had gone before. Built on the site where Melchizedek had offered bread and wine, and where Abraham had offered his son, and where God had sworn His oath to save all nations, the Temple served as the enduring place of offerings, principal of which was identical with that most ancient sacrifice of Abel: the lamb.

For the great day of sacrifice remained the feast of Passover, when as many as two and a half million pilgrims thronged Jerusalem, coming from the far corners of the known world. The first-century Jewish historian Josephus records that, on Passover in the year A.D. 70—only months before the Romans destroyed the Temple, and some forty years after Jesus' ascension—the priests offered more than a quarter of a million lambs on the Temple's altar—256,500, to be precise.

INSIDE AND OUT

Was all of this sacrifice merely empty ritual? No, although the burnt offering, by itself, was clearly not enough. God demanded an *interior* sacrifice as well. The psalmist declared that "The sacrifice acceptable to God is a broken spirit" (Ps 51:17). The prophet Hosea spoke for God, saying, "I desire steadfast love and not sacrifice, the knowledge of God, rather than burnt offerings" (Hos 6:6).

Yet the obligation to offer sacrifice remained. We know that Jesus observed the Jewish laws regarding sacrifice. He celebrated the Passover every year in Jerusalem; and presumably He ate the sacrificed lamb, first with His family and later with His Apostles. After all, it wasn't optional. Consuming the lamb was the only way a faithful Jew could renew his covenant with God, and Jesus was a faithful Jew.

But Passover had more than an ordinary importance

in Jesus' life; it was central to His mission, a definitive moment. Jesus *is* the Lamb. When Jesus stood before Pilate, John notes that "it was the day of preparation of the Passover; it was about the sixth hour" (19:14). John knew that the sixth hour was when the priests were beginning to slaughter the Passover lambs. This, then, is the moment of the sacrifice of the Lamb of God.

Next, John recounts that none of Jesus' bones were broken on the cross, "that the Scripture might be fulfilled" (19:36). Which Scripture was that? Exodus 12:46, which stipulates that the Passover lamb must have no broken bones. We see, then, that the Lamb of God, like the Passover lamb, is a worthy offering, a perfect fulfillment.

In the same passage, John relates that the onlookers served Jesus sour wine from a sponge on a hyssop branch (see Jn 19:29; Ex 12:22). Hyssop was the branch prescribed by the Law for the Passover sprinkling of the lamb's blood. Thus, this simple action marked the fulfillment of the new and perfect redemption. And Jesus cried out, "It is finished."

Finally, in speaking of Jesus' garment at the time of the crucifixion, John uses the precise term for the vestments the high priest wore when he offered sacrifices such as the Passover lamb.

VICTIM'S RITES

What can we conclude from this? John makes it clear to us that, *in the new and definitive Passover sacrifice, Jesus is both priest and victim.* This is confirmed in the other three Gospels' accounts of the Last Supper, where Jesus clearly uses the priestly language of sacrifice and libations, even as He describes Himself as the victim. "This is My body which is given for you. . . . This cup which is poured out for you is the new covenant in My blood" (Lk 22:19–20).

Jesus' sacrifice would accomplish what all the blood of millions of sheep and bulls and goats could never do. "For it is impossible that the blood of bulls and goats should take away sins" (Heb 10:4). Even the blood of a quarter of a million lambs could not save the nation of Israel, never mind the world. To atone for offenses against a God Who is all-good, infinite, and eternal, mankind needed a perfect sacrifice: a sacrifice as good and unblemished and boundless as God Himself. And that was Jesus, Who alone could "put away sin by the sacrifice of Himself" (Heb 9:26).

"Behold the Lamb of God!" (Jn 1:36). Why did Jesus have to be a lamb, and not a stallion or a tiger or a bull? Why does Revelation portray Jesus as a "lamb standing as if slain" (Rev 5:6)? Why must the Mass proclaim Him as the "Lamb of God"? Because only a sacrificial lamb fits the divine pattern of our salvation.

Moreover, Jesus was priest as well as victim, and as priest He could do what no other high priest could do. For the high priest entered "the Holy Place yearly with blood not his own" (Heb 9:25), and even then stayed only briefly before his unworthiness drove him out. But Jesus entered the holiest of holies—heaven—once for all, to offer Himself as our sacrifice. What is more, by Jesus' new Passover, we, too, have been made a kingdom of priests and the Church of the firstborn (see Rev 1:6; Heb 12:23, and compare to Ex 4:22 and 19:6); and with Him we enter heaven's sanctuary, whenever we go to Mass. We'll revisit all these images later on, when we see that holiest of holies in the Book of Revelation, with its altar, and its Temple, its incense, and its omnipresent Lamb.

DON'T PASS OVER THIS FEAST

But what does this mean to us today? How should we celebrate our Passover? St. Paul gives us a clue: "Christ, our paschal lamb, has been sacrificed. Let us, therefore celebrate the festival . . . with the unleavened bread of sincerity and truth" (1 Cor 5:7–8). Our Passover lamb, then, is unleavened bread. Our festival is the Mass (see 1 Cor 10:15–21; 11:23–32).

In the clear light of the New Covenant, the Old Covenant sacrifices make sense as preparation for the one sacrifice of Jesus Christ, our royal high priest in the heavenly sanctuary. And it is this one sacrifice we offer, with Jesus, in the Mass. In this light, we see the prayers of the Mass with new clarity.

We offer You His body and blood, the acceptable sacrifice which brings salvation to the whole world. Lord, look upon this sacrifice which You have given to Your Church . . . *(Eucharistic Prayer IV).*

[F]rom the many gifts You have given us we offer to You, God of glory and majesty, this holy and perfect sacrifice. . . . Look with favor on these offerings and accept them as once You accepted the gifts of Your servant Abel, the sacrifice of Abraham, our father in faith, and the bread and wine offered by Your priest Melchizedek. Almighty God, we pray that Your angel may take this sacrifice to Your altar in heaven *(Eucharistic Prayer I)*.

It is not enough that Christ bled and died for our sake. Now we have our part to play. As with the Old Covenant, so with the New. If you want to mark your covenant with God, to seal your covenant with God, to renew your covenant with God, *you have to eat the Lamb*—the paschal lamb Who is our unleavened bread. It begins to sound familiar. "Unless you eat the flesh of the Son of man and drink His blood, you have no life in you" (Jn 6:54).

RETURN ON INVESTMENT

Man's primal need to worship God has always expressed itself in sacrifice: worship that is simultaneously an act of praise, atonement, self-giving, covenant, and thanksgiving (in Greek, *eucharistia)*. The various forms of sacrifice have one common, positive meaning: life is surrendered in order to be transformed and shared. So when Jesus spoke of His life as a sacrifice, He tapped into a current running deep in the souls of His Apostles—running deep in the souls of Israelites—running deep in every human soul. In the twentieth century, Mohandas Gandhi, who was a Hindu, called "worship without sacrifice" an absurdity of the modern age. But worship is not so for Catholics. Our supreme act of worship is a supreme act of sacrifice: the Lamb's Supper, the Mass.

Sacrifice is a need of the human heart. But, until Jesus, no sacrifice would suffice. Remember Psalm

116:12: "How shall I make a return to the Lord for all the good He has done for me?" How, indeed?

God knew all along what our answer would be. "The cup of salvation I will take up, and I will call upon the name of the Lord" (Ps 116:13).

THREE

From the Beginning

THE MASS OF THE FIRST
CHRISTIANS

CANNIBALISM" and "human sacrifice" were charges often whispered against the first generations of Christians. The early Christian apologists took them up in order to dismiss them as gossip. Yet through the distorted lens of the pagans' gossip, we can see what was the most identifiable element of Christian life and worship.

It was the Eucharist: the re-presentation of the sacrifice of Jesus Christ, the sacramental meal where Christians consumed Jesus' body and blood. It was the distortion of these facts of faith that led to pagan calumnies against the Church—though it's easy to see how the pagans misunderstood. In the early Church, only the baptized were permitted to attend the sacraments, and Christians were discouraged from even discussing these central mysteries with non-Christians. So the pagan imagination was left to run wild, fueled by small scraps of fact: "this is My body . . . this is the cup of My blood . . . Unless you eat the flesh of the Son of man and drink His blood . . ." The pagans knew that to be a Christian was to participate in some strange and secretive rites.

To be a Christian was to go to Mass. This was true from the first day of the New Covenant. Just hours after Jesus rose from the dead, He found His way to a table with two disciples. "He took the bread and blessed, and broke it, and gave it to them. And their eyes were opened . . . He was known to them in the breaking of the bread" (Lk 24:30–31, 35). The centrality of the Eucharist is evident also in the Acts of the Apostles' capsule description of the early Church's life: "They devoted themselves to the Apostles' teaching and fellowship, to the breaking of bread and the prayers" (Acts 2:42). St. Paul's First Letter to the Corinthians (ch. 11) contains a veritable handbook of liturgical theory and practice. Paul's letter reveals his concern to transmit the precise form of the liturgy, in the words of institution taken from Jesus' Last Supper. "For I received from the Lord what I also delivered to you, that the Lord Jesus on the night when He was betrayed took bread, and when He had given thanks, He broke it, and said, 'This is My body which is for you. Do this in remembrance of Me.' In the same way also the cup, after supper, saying, 'This cup is the new covenant in My blood. Do this, as often as you drink it, in remembrance of Me' " (1 Cor 11:23–25). Paul emphasizes the importance of the doctrine of the Real Presence and sees dire consequences in unbelief: "Any one who eats and drinks without discerning the body eats and drinks judgment upon himself" (1 Cor 11:29).

GUIDED MISSAL

We note the same themes as we move from the New Testament books to other Christian sources from the age of the Apostles and immediately afterward. The doctrinal content is identical, and the vocabulary remains remarkably similar, even as the faith spread to other lands and other languages. The clergy, teachers, and defenders of the early Church were united in their concern to preserve the Eucharistic doctrines: the Real Presence of Jesus' body and blood under the appearance of bread and wine; the sacrificial nature of the liturgy; the necessity of properly ordained clergy; the importance of ritual form. Thus, the witness to the Church's Eucharistic doctrines is unbroken, from the time of the Gospels till today.

Aside from the books of the New Testament, the earliest Christian writing that has survived is a liturgical manual—what we might call a missal—contained within a document called the *Didache* (Greek for "Teaching"). The *Didache* claims to be the collected "Teaching of the Apostles," and was likely compiled in Antioch, Syria (see Acts 11:26), sometime during the years A.D. 50–110. The *Didache* uses the word "sacrifice" four times to describe the Eucharist, once stating plainly that "this is the sacrifice that was spoken of by the Lord." From the *Didache* we also learn that the usual day of the liturgy was "the Lord's

day" and that it was customary to repent of one's sins
before receiving the Eucharist. "On the Lord's own day
gather yourselves together and break bread and give
thanks, first confessing your transgressions, that your sacrifice may be pure." As for the order of the sacrifice, the
Didache offers a Eucharistic Prayer that is stunning in its
poetry. We can find its echoes in liturgies and hymns of
Christians today, both Eastern and Western:

> As this broken bread was scattered upon the mountains
> and, gathered together, became one, so may Your Church
> be gathered together from the ends of the earth into Your
> kingdom; for Yours is the glory and the power through
> Jesus Christ for ever and ever. But let no one eat or drink
> of this Eucharistic thanksgiving, except those who have
> been baptized into the name of the Lord. . . .
>
> Almighty Master, You created all things for Your
> name's sake, and gave food and drink to men for enjoy-
> ment, that they might give thanks to You; but You be-
> stowed upon us spiritual food and drink and eternal life
> through Your Son. . . .
>
> Remember, Lord, Your Church. Deliver it from all
> evil and perfect it in Your love; and gather it together
> from the four winds—the Church that has been sancti-
> fied—into Your kingdom which You have prepared for it.

ROOTS IN ISRAEL

The liturgy of the ancient Church drew deeply from the
rites and the Scriptures of ancient Israel, as does our own
liturgy today. In Chapter 2, we considered how Jesus insti-

tuted the Mass during the feast of Passover. His "thanks-giving"—His Eucharist—would fulfill, perfect, and surpass the Passover sacrifice. This connection was clear to the first generation of Christians, many of whom were devout Jews. Thus the prayers of Passover soon found their way into the Christian liturgy.

Consider the prayers over the wine and the unleavened bread in the Passover meal: "Blessed are You, Lord our God, Creator of the fruit of the vine. . . . Blessed are You, Lord our God, King of the universe, Who brings forth bread from the earth." The phrase "Holy, holy, holy is the Lord of Hosts! The earth is full of His glory" (Is 6:3) was another commonplace of Jewish worship, which found its way immediately into Christian rites. We will encounter it in the Book of Revelation, but it also appears in a letter composed by the fourth pope, St. Clement of Rome, around the year A.D. 96.

TODAH RECALL

Perhaps the most striking liturgical "ancestor" of the Mass is the *todah* of ancient Israel. The Hebrew word *todah,* like the Greek Eucharist, means "thank offering" or "thanksgiving." The word denotes a sacrificial meal shared with friends in order to celebrate one's gratitude to God. A *todah* begins by recalling some mortal threat and then celebrates man's divine deliverance from that threat. It is a powerful expression of confidence in God's sovereignty and mercy.

Psalm 69 is a good example. An urgent plea for deliverance ("Save me, O God!"), it is at the same time a celebration of that eventual deliverance ("I will praise the name of God with a song . . . For the Lord hears the needy").

Perhaps the classic example of the *todah* is Psalm 22, which begins with "My God, my God, why have You forsaken me?" Jesus Himself quoted this as He hung dying upon the cross. His listeners would have recognized the reference, and they would have known that this song, which begins with a cry of dereliction, ends on a triumphant note of salvation. Citing this *todah*, Jesus demonstrated His own confident hope for deliverance.

The similarities between *todah* and Eucharist go beyond their common meaning of thanksgiving. Cardinal Joseph Ratzinger has written: "Structurally speaking, the whole of Christology, indeed the whole of Eucharistic Christology, is present in the *todah* spirituality of the Old Testament." Both the *todah* and the Eucharist present their worship through word and meal. Moreover, the *todah*, like the Mass, includes an unbloody offering of unleavened bread and wine.

The ancient rabbis made a significant prediction regarding the *todah*. "In the coming [Messianic] age, all sacrifices will cease except the *todah* sacrifice. This will never cease in all eternity" *(Pesiqta,* I, p. 159).

ACCEPT NO SUBSTITUTES

From Antioch, in Syria, again comes our next witness to the newborn Church's Eucharistic doctrine. Around A.D. 107, St. Ignatius, bishop of Antioch, wrote often of the Eucharist as he traveled westward to his martyrdom. He speaks of the Church as "the place of sacrifice." And to the Philadelphians he wrote: "Take care, then, to have but one Eucharist. For there is one flesh of our Lord Jesus Christ, and one cup to show forth the unity of His blood; one altar, as there is one bishop, along with the priests and deacons, my fellow-servants." In his letter to the Church of Smyrna, Ignatius lashed out against heretics who, even at that early date, were denying the true doctrine: "From the Eucharist and prayer they hold aloof, because they do not confess that the Eucharist is the flesh of our Savior Jesus Christ." He counsels readers on the marks of a true liturgy: "Let that be deemed a proper Eucharist which is administered either by the bishop or by one to whom he has entrusted it."

Ignatius spoke of the sacrament with a realism that must have been shocking to people unfamiliar with the mysteries of Christian faith. Surely it was words like his, taken out of context, that fed the Roman Empire's gossip mills, which in turn spewed out the charges of cannibalism. In the following decades, the Church's defense fell to a scholarly convert from Samaria named Justin. It was Justin who lifted the veil of secrecy over the ancient liturgy. In A.D. 155, he wrote to the Roman emperor describing what we can, even now, recognize as the Mass. It's worth quoting at length:

> On the day we call the day of the sun, all who dwell in the city or country gather in the same place. The memoirs of the apostles and the writings of the prophets are read, as much as time permits. When the reader has finished, he who presides over those gathered admonishes and chal-

lenges them to imitate these beautiful things. Then we all rise together and offer prayers for ourselves . . . and for all others, wherever they may be, so that we may be found righteous by our life and actions, and faithful to the commandments, so as to obtain eternal salvation. When the prayers are concluded we exchange the kiss. Then someone brings bread and a cup of water and wine mixed together to him who presides over the brethren. He takes them and offers praise and glory to the Father of the universe, through the name of the Son and of the Holy Spirit and for a considerable time he gives thanks (in Greek: *eucharistian)* that we have been judged worthy of these gifts. When he has concluded the prayers and thanksgivings, all present give voice to an acclamation by saying: "Amen." When he who presides has given thanks and the people have responded, those whom we call deacons give to those present the "eucharisted" bread, wine and water and take them to those who are absent.

Justin begins his description by placing it squarely on "the day of the sun"—Sunday, which was the day Jesus rose from the dead. This identification of "the Lord's day" with Sunday is the universal testimony of the early Christians. As the primary day of worship, Sunday had fulfilled and replaced the seventh day, the sabbath of the Jews. It was the Lord's day, for example, when John, worshiping "in the Spirit," had his vision of the Apocalypse (Rev 1:10).

TEXT AND GRAPHICS

Justin explains the Church's sacrifice and sacrament. Yet he does not downplay the Real Presence. He uses the same graphic realism as his predecessor, Ignatius: "The food that has been made the Eucharist by the prayer of His word, and which nourishes our flesh and blood by assimilation, is both the flesh and blood of that Jesus Who was made flesh."

When speaking with Jews, Justin went further and explained that the Passover sacrifice and the Temple sacrifices were mere foreshadowings of the one sacrifice of Jesus Christ and its re-presentation in the liturgy: "And the offering of fine flour . . . which was prescribed to be presented on behalf of those purified from leprosy, was a type of the bread of the Eucharist, the celebration of which our Lord Jesus Christ prescribed."

Such was the *catholic,* or universal, experience of the Eucharist. Yet, while the doctrine remained the same throughout the world, the liturgy was, for the most part, a local affair. Each bishop was responsible for the celebration of the Eucharist in his territory, and, gradually, different regions developed their own styles of liturgical practice: Syrian, Roman, Gallican, and so on. What is remarkable, however, is how much all these liturgies—widely varied as they were—kept in common. With few exceptions, they shared the same basic elements: a rite of repentance, readings from the Scriptures, the singing or recitation of psalms, a homily, an "angelic hymn," a Eucharistic Prayer, and Holy Communion. The churches followed St. Paul in taking special care to transmit the words of institution, the words that transform the bread and wine into the body and blood of Christ: "This is My body . . . This is the cup of My blood."

THAT OLD FAMILIAR REFRAIN

From the beginning of the third century onward, the papyrus trail shows a greater concern with preserving the precise words of the liturgies attributed to the Apostles. In the early 300s A.D., in northern Syria, surfaces another compilation of the received tradition: the *Didascalia Apostolorum* ("Teaching of the Apostles"). The *Didascalia* includes pages of texts of prayers as well as detailed instructions for the liturgical roles and etiquette of bishops, priests, deacons, women, children, young adults, widows, orphans, and travelers.

Around A.D. 215, Hippolytus of Rome composed his great work, *The Apostolic Tradition,* in which he set down the liturgical and theological teachings the Roman Church had preserved from the days of the Apostles. One section sets out a tightly scripted liturgy for the ordination of priests. Whereas in Justin's description we can "see" our Mass, in Hippolytus's work we can *hear* it.

PRIEST: The Lord be with you.
CONGREGATION: And with your spirit.
PRIEST: Let us lift up our hearts.
CONGREGATION: We lift them up to the Lord.

PRIEST: Let us give thanks to the Lord.
CONGREGATION: It is right and just.

From the same period, we find the oldest texts of the liturgies that claimed apostolic lineage, the liturgies of St. Mark, St. James, and St. Peter—liturgies still used in many places throughout the world. The liturgy of St. James was the favored rite of the ancient Jerusalem Church, which claimed James as its first bishop. The liturgies of James, Mark, and Peter are theologically dense, rich in poetry, rich in citations from the Scriptures. Remember, since few people could read, and still fewer could afford to have books copied out, the liturgy was the place where Christians absorbed the Bible. So, from the Church's earliest days, the Mass has been saturated with the Scriptures.

Though their words speak eloquently of Christ's sacrifice, the ancient liturgies are just as resounding in their silences:

Let all mortal flesh keep silence,
and stand with fear and trembling,
and meditate nothing earthly within itself.
For the King of kings and Lord of lords,
Christ our God, comes forward to be sacrificed,
and to be given for food to the faithful.
And the bands of angels go before Him
with every power and dominion,
the many-eyed cherubim, and the six-winged seraphim,
covering their faces, and crying aloud the hymn:
Alleluia, Alleluia, Alleluia.

Keep all of this in mind: the sounds and the silences of the Church's first Masses. You'll encounter them again in heaven, when we examine the Book of Revelation more closely. You'll encounter them again in heaven, when you go to Mass next Sunday.

FOUR

Taste and See (and Hear and Touch) the Gospel

UNDERSTANDING THE PARTS OF THE MASS

SOME PEOPLE, romantics at heart, like to think that early Christian worship was purely spontaneous and improvised. They like to imagine the first believers so overflowing with enthusiasm that praise and thanksgiving just overflowed into profound prayer as the Church gathered to break bread. After all, who needs a missal in order to shout "I love you"?

Once I believed that. Study of the Scriptures and Tradition, however, led me to see the good sense of order in worship. Gradually, I found myself (while still a Protestant) drawn to liturgy and trying to construct a liturgy out of the words of Scripture. Little did I know it had already been done.

As early as St. Paul, we see the Church's concern with ritual precision and liturgical etiquette. I believe there's good reason for this. I beg the patience of my romantic

where?,

friends as I say that order and routine are not necessarily bad things. In fact, they are indispensable to a good, godly, and peaceful life. Without schedules and routines, we could accomplish little in our workday. Without set phrases, what would our human relationships be? I've yet to meet parents who tire of hearing their children repeat that ancient phrase, "Thank you." I've yet to meet the spouse who's sick of hearing "I love you."

Faithfulness to our routines is a way of showing love. We don't just work, or thank, or offer affection when we really feel like it. Real loves are loves we live with constancy, and that constancy shows itself in routine.

LITURGY IS HABIT-FORMING

Routines are not just good theory. They work in practice. Order makes life more peaceful, more efficient, and more effective. In fact the more routines we develop, the more effective we become. Routines free us from the need to ponder small details over and over again; routines let good habits take over, freeing the mind and heart to move onward and upward.

The rites of the Christian liturgy are the set phrases that have proven themselves over time: the thank-you of God's children, the I-love-you of Christ's spouse, the Church. The liturgy is the habit that makes us highly effective, not just in "spiritual life," but in life generally, since life must be lived in a world that's made and redeemed by God.

Liturgy engages the whole person: body, soul, and spirit. I remember the first time I attended a Catholic liturgical event, a vespers service at a Byzantine seminary. My Calvinist background and training had not prepared me for the experience—the incense and icons, the prostrations and bows, the chant and the bells. All my senses were taken up. Afterward a seminarian asked me, "What do you think?" All I could say was, "Now I know why God gave me a body: to worship the Lord with His people in liturgy." Catholics don't just hear the Gospel. In the liturgy, we hear, see, smell, and taste it.

HALVING A GOOD TIME

We hear the call of Mass most clearly perhaps in a phrase that echoes throughout most of the world's liturgies, through all of the Church's history: Lift up your hearts! Where are our hearts going? To heaven, because the Mass is heaven on earth. Yet, before we can see this clearly (and here's a secret: before we can understand the Book of Revelation), we have to understand the parts of the Mass.

In this chapter, we'll walk step by step through the liturgy to see how each element "works"—where it comes from and what it's for. Though we have space to treat only a few of the major details, these should be enough to help us begin to contemplate the Mass, and begin to discover its inner logic. For, unless we understand both the parts and the whole, the Mass *can* become mindless routine, without heartfelt participation; and that's the sort of routine that gives routine a bad name.

First, we should understand that the Mass is really divided in two: the "Liturgy of the Word" and the "Lit-

very true ✳

urgy of the Eucharist." These halves are further divided into specific rituals. In the Latin Church, the Liturgy of the Word includes the entrance, the introductory rites, the penitential rite, and the readings from Scripture. The Liturgy of the Eucharist could be marked off in four sections: the offertory, the Eucharistic Prayer, the Communion rite, and the concluding rite. Though the actions are many, the Mass is *one offering*, and that is the sacrifice of Jesus Christ, which renews our covenant with God the Father.

CROSS PURPOSES

Among the early Christians, the Sign of the Cross was probably the most universal expression of faith. It appears often in the documents of the period. In most places, the custom was simply to trace the cross upon the forehead. Some writers (such as St. Jerome and St. Augustine) describe Christians tracing the cross on the forehead, then the lips, and then the heart, as modern Western Catholics do just before the reading of the Gospel. Great saints also testify to the tremendous power of the sign. St. Cyprian of Carthage, in the third century, wrote that "in the . . . Sign of the Cross is all virtue and power. . . . In this Sign of the Cross is salvation for all who are marked on their foreheads" (a reference, by the way, to Revelation 7:3 and 14:1). A century later, St. Athanasius declared that "by the Sign of the Cross all magic is stopped, and all witchcraft brought to nothing." Satan is powerless before the cross of Jesus Christ.

The Sign of the Cross is the most profound gesture

we make. It is the mystery of the Gospel in a moment. It is the Christian faith summarized in a single gesture. When we cross ourselves, we renew the covenant that began with our baptism. With our words, we proclaim the Trinitarian faith into which we were baptized ("In the name of the Father, and of the Son, and of the Holy Spirit"). With our hand, we proclaim our redemption by the cross of Jesus Christ. The greatest sin of human history—the crucifixion of the Son of God—became the greatest act of merciful love and divine power. The cross is the means by which we are saved, by which we become partakers in the divine nature (see 2 Pet 1:4). *okay, I see the connection.*

(his glory + goodness)

Trinity, incarnation, redemption—the entire creed flashes in that brief moment. In the East, the gesture is richer still, as Christians trace the sign holding the first three fingers together (thumb, index, middle) apart from the other two (ring and pinkie): the three fingers together represent the unity of the Trinity; the two fingers together represent the union of Christ's two natures, human and divine.

This is not only an act of worship. It is also a reminder of who we are. "Father, Son, and Holy Spirit" reflects a family relationship, the inner life and eternal communion of God. Ours is the only religion whose one God is a family. God Himself is an "eternal family"; but, because of our baptism, He is *our* family, too. Baptism is a sacrament, which comes from the Latin word for oath *(sacramentum);* and by this oath we are bound to the family of God. By making the Sign of the Cross, we begin the Mass with a reminder that we are children of God.

We also renew the solemn oath of our baptism. Making the Sign of the Cross, then, is like swearing on the Bible in a court of law. We promise that we have come to Mass to offer testimony. So we are not spectators in worship; we are active participants, we are witnesses, and we swear to tell the truth, the whole truth, and nothing but the truth. So help us, God.

A RITE FOR WRONGS

If we're on the witness stand, then who's on trial? The Penitential Rite makes it clear: We are. The earliest liturgical guidelines we have, the *Didache,* say that an act of confession should precede our participation in the Eucharist. The beautiful thing about the Mass, though, is that no one rises to accuse us but we ourselves. "I confess to Almighty God . . . that I have sinned through my own fault."

We have sinned. We can't deny that. "If we say, 'We are without sin,' we deceive ourselves, and the truth is not in us" (1 Jn 1:9). Moreover, says the Good Book, even the just man falls seven times a day (see Prov 24:16). We are no exceptions, and honesty demands that we acknowledge our guilt. Even our small sins are serious matters because each one is an offense against a God Whose greatness is unmeasurable. So, in the Mass, we plead guilty and then throw ourselves on the mercy of heaven's court. In the *Kyrie,* we ask mercy of each of the three divine persons in the Trinity: "Lord, have mercy. Christ, have mercy. Lord, have mercy." We don't make excuses or rationalize. We ask forgiveness and we hear the message of mercy. If one word captures the meaning of the Mass, it's "mercy."

The phrase "Lord, have mercy" appears often in Scripture, in both testaments (see, for example, Ps 6:2, 31:9; Mt 15:22, 17:15, 20:30). The Old Testament teaches again and again that mercy is among God's greatest attributes (see Ex 34:6; Jon 4:2).

The "Lord, have mercy" has endured since the earliest Christian liturgies. In fact, even in the Latin West it is often preserved in the more ancient Greek form: *Kyrie, eleison*. In some liturgies of the East, the congregation repeats the *Kyrie* in response to a longer litany begging favors from God. Among the Byzantines, these petitions overwhelmingly ask for peace: "In peace, let us pray to the Lord . . . For peace from on high . . . For peace in the whole world . . ."

G-L-O-R-I-A

We pray for peace, and within seconds we proclaim our prayer's fulfillment: "Glory to God in the highest and peace to His people on earth." This prayer has been around since at least the second century. Its opening acclamation comes from the song the angels sang at Jesus' birth (Lk 2:14), and the following lines echo the angels' praises of God's power from the Book of Revelation (especially Rev 15:3–4).

We praise God immediately for the blessings we just prayed for. That's our testimony of God's power. That's His glory. Jesus said: "Whatever you ask in My name, I will do it, that the Father may be glorified in the Son; if you ask anything in My name, I will do it" (Jn 14:13–14). The Gloria cries out with the joy, confidence, and hope that have always marked believers. In the Gloria, the Mass is reminiscent of the Old Covenant *todah,* which we discussed earlier. Our sacrifice is an urgent plea for deliverance, but at the same time it is a celebration and thanksgiving for that deliverance. That's the faith of someone who knows God's providential care. That's the Gloria.

THE FULL-GOSPEL CHURCH

The defining moment of the Liturgy of the Word is, of course, the proclamation of the Word of God. On Sundays, this will usually include an Old Testament reading, the singing or recitation of a Psalm, and a reading from the New Testament letters, all of which builds to the reading of the Gospel. (On Easter Vigil, we get as many as ten sizable readings from the Bible.) All told, that's a powerhouse of Scripture. Catholics who attend Mass daily hear almost the entire Bible read to them in the course of three years—and then there are the veins of Scriptural gold embedded in all the other prayers of the Mass. . . . Don't ever let people tell you that the Church doesn't call Catholics to be "Bible Christians."

In fact, the Bible's "natural habitat" is in the liturgy. "Faith comes by hearing," St. Paul said (Rom 10:17). Notice that he did *not* say, "Faith comes by reading." In the early centuries of the Church, there were no printing presses. Most people could not afford to have the Gospels

[47]

[handwritten margin note: maybe not but faith can grow thru daily reading]

copied out by hand, and many people couldn't read anyway. So where did Christians receive the Gospel? In the Mass—and then, as now, they got the full Gospel.

The readings you hear at Mass are preprogrammed for a three-year cycle in a book called the *lectionary*. This book is an effective antidote to a tendency I had, as a Protestant preacher, to target my favorite texts and preach on them again and again. I could go years without touching some of the books of the Old Testament. This should never be a problem for Catholics who regularly attend Mass.

We can't be too attentive during the readings. They are a normal and essential preparation for our Holy Communion with Jesus. One of the great Scripture scholars of the early Church, Origen (third century), urged Christians to respect Christ's presence in the Gospel as they respect His presence in the Host.

> You who are accustomed to take part in the divine mysteries know, when you receive the body of the Lord, how you protect it with all caution and veneration lest any small part fall from it, lest anything of the consecrated gift be lost. For you believe, and correctly, that you are answerable if anything falls from there by neglect. But if you are so careful to preserve His body, and rightly so, how do you think that there is less guilt to have neglected God's word than to have neglected His body?

Seventeen centuries later, the Second Vatican Council echoed this ancient teaching for our own time: "The

Church has always venerated the divine Scriptures just as she venerates the body of the Lord, since, especially in the sacred liturgy, she unceasingly receives and offers to the faithful the bread of life from the table both of God's word and of Christ's body" *(Dei Verbum* 21).

"No one," said Origen, "understands in heart . . . unless he be open-minded and totally intent." Does that describe you and me when we hear the readings at Mass? We need to be particularly attentive during the readings because, from the beginning of the Mass, you and I are under oath. By receiving the Word—which, we acknowledge, comes from God—we are agreeing to be bound by the Word. As a result, we are liable to judgment depending on how well we live up to the readings of the Mass. In the Old Covenant, to hear the Law was to agree to live by the Law—or receive the curses that came with disobedience. In the New Covenant, too, we are bound by what we hear, as we'll see in the Book of Revelation.

THE NEED TO HEED THE CREED

The Liturgy of the Word proceeds, on Sundays, to the homily (or sermon) and the creed. In the homily, the priest or deacon offers us a commentary on God's inspired word. Homilies should draw from the Scriptures of the day, lighting up the obscure passages and pointing out practical applications for ordinary life. Homilies don't have to entertain us. Just as Jesus comes to us in humble, tasteless wafers, so the Holy Spirit sometimes works through a monotone, lackluster preacher.

After the homily, we recite the Nicene Creed, which is the faith distilled into just a few lines. The words of the creed are precise, with diamond-like clarity and cut. Compared to prayers like the Gloria, the Nicene Creed appears dispassionate, but appearances can be deceptive. As the late, great Dorothy Sayers said, the drama is in the dogma. For here we proclaim doctrines for which Christian citizens of the Roman Empire suffered imprisonment and death. In the fourth century, the empire nearly exploded into civil war over the doctrines of Jesus' divinity and His oneness with the Father. New heresies arose and spread like a cancer through the Church, threatening the life of the body. It took the great councils of Nicaea (325) and Constantinople (381)—engaging some of the greatest minds and souls in Church history—to give basic Catholic belief this definitive formulation, though most of the lines of the creed had been in common usage since at least the third century. After those councils, many churches in the East required the faithful to *sing* the creed every week—not just recite it—because this was indeed good news, lifesaving news.

Cardinal Joseph Ratzinger has stated the connection between Gospel and creed succinctly: "Dogma is by definition nothing other than an interpretation of Scripture . . . which has sprung from the faith over the centuries." The creed is the "faith of our fathers" that is "living still." Likewise, the International Theological Commission's 1989 document "On the Interpretation of Dogmas" states: "In the dogma of the Church one is thus concerned with the correct interpretation of the Scrip-

true →

tures. . . . A later time cannot reverse that which was formulated under the assistance of the Holy Spirit as a key for the reading of the Scriptures." When we recite the creed on Sunday, we publicly accept this scriptural faith as objective truth. We enter the drama of the dogma, for which our ancestors were willing to die.

We join these ancestors, then, as we recite the "prayers of the faithful," our petitions. The creed empowers us to enter into the intercessory ministry of the saints. At this point, the Liturgy of the Word comes to an end, and we enter the mysteries of the Eucharist.

GIVE HIM AN OFFERING HE CAN'T REFUSE

The Liturgy of the Eucharist starts with the offertory, and the offertory bespeaks our commitment. We bring bread, wine, and money to support the Church's work. In the early Church, the faithful actually baked the bread and pressed the wine for the celebration; at the offertory they brought it forward. (In some Eastern churches, the bread and wine are still produced by the parishioners.) The point is this: We offer ourselves and all that we have. Not because we're so special, but because we know the Lord can take what is temporal and make it eternal, take what is human and make it divine. The Second Vatican Council spoke powerfully of the offering of the laity: "[T]heir work, prayers and apostolic endeavors, their ordinary married and family life, their daily labor, their mental and physical relaxation . . . all of these become spiritual sacrifices acceptable to God through Jesus Christ. During

interesting

the celebration of the Eucharist these sacrifices are most lovingly offered to the Father along with the Lord's body. Thus as worshipers whose every deed is holy, the lay faithful consecrate the world itself to God" *(Lumen Gentium 34)*.

Okay → Everything we have goes on the altar, to be made holy in Christ. The priest makes the connection explicit as he pours the water and wine into the chalices: "By the mystery of this water and wine, may we come to share in the divinity of Christ, Who humbled Himself to share in our humanity." This mingling is a rich symbol, suggesting the union of Christ's divine and human nature, the blood and water that poured forth from His side on the cross, and the union of our own gifts with the Savior's perfect gift of Himself. That's an offer the Father cannot refuse.

UPWARD MOBILITY

Now, as the priest has lifted up the gifts, he invites us to "Lift up your hearts." This is a powerful image, and you'll find it in Christian liturgies throughout the world and since the earliest times. We lift our hearts to heaven. In the words of the Apocalypse (see Rev 1:10; 4:1–2), we are taken up in the spirit—to heaven. From now on, we are saying, we will look at reality by faith and not by sight.

Cool! So what do we see in this heaven? We recognize that all around us are the angels and the saints. We sing the song that, according to many accounts, the angels and saints sing before heaven's throne (see Rev 4:8; Is 6:2–3). In the West we call it the "Sanctus," or "Holy, Holy,

Holy''; in the East, it's the "Trisagion," or "Thrice-Holy Hymn."

Then comes the climax of the Eucharistic sacrifice, the great Eucharistic Prayer (or Anaphora). This is where it becomes clear that the New Covenant is not a book. It's an action, and that action is the Eucharist. There are many Eucharistic Prayers in use throughout the Church, but all contain the same elements:

what?

- *The Epiclesis.* This is when the priest places his hands over the gifts and calls down the Holy Spirit. This is a powerful encounter with heaven, more richly appreciated in the East.
- *The Narrative of Institution* is the moment when the Spirit and the Word transform the elements from bread and wine into the body and blood, soul and divinity of Jesus Christ. Now, the priest relates the drama of the Last Supper, when Jesus made provision for the renewal of His covenant sacrifice through all time. What Exodus 12 was to the Passover liturgy, the Gospels are for the Eucharistic Prayer—but with a major difference. The words of the new Passover "effect what they signify." When the priest speaks the words of institution—"This is My body . . . This is the cup of My blood, the blood of the new and everlasting covenant"—he is not merely narrating, he is speaking *in the person of Christ,* Who is the principal celebrant of the Mass. By the sacrament of Holy Orders, a man is changed in his very being; as priest, he becomes "another Christ." Jesus ordained the Apostles and their successors to celebrate the Mass when He said: "Do

what?

what's that?

obviously

this . . . in remembrance of Me" (1 Cor 11:25). Note that Jesus commanded them to *"do* this," and not "write this" or "read this."

- *Remembrance.* We use the English words "Remembrance" and "Memory" to describe the next section of the Eucharistic Prayer, but these words hardly do justice to the terms in the original language. In the Old Testament, for example, we often read that God "remembered His covenant." Well, it's not as if He could ever forget His covenant; but at certain times, for the benefit of His people, He renewed it, He re-presented it, He reenacted it. That's what He does, through His priest, in the remembrance of the Mass. He makes His New Covenant new once again.

what's she trying to say here?

- *Offering.* The Mass's "memory" is not imaginary. It has flesh; it is Jesus in His glorified humanity, and He is our offering. "Father, calling to mind the death Your Son endured for our salvation . . . we offer You in thanksgiving this holy and living sacrifice" *(Eucharistic Prayer III).*

- *Intercessions.* Then, with Jesus Himself, we pray to the Father for the living and the dead, for the whole Church and the whole world.

did not know that!

- *Doxology.* The end of the Eucharistic Prayer is a dramatic moment. We call it a "doxology," which is Greek for "word of glory." The priest lifts up the chalice and the host, which he now refers to as *Him.* This is Jesus, and "Through Him, with Him, in Him, all glory and honor is Yours, almighty Father, forever and ever." Our "Amen!" here should be resounding; it is traditionally called "The Great Amen." In the fourth cen-

tury, St. Jerome reported that, in Rome, when the
Great Amen was proclaimed, all the pagan temples
trembled.

[handwritten: who?]

FAMILY MATTERS

We follow the Eucharistic Prayer with the Our Father, the
prayer that Jesus taught us. We find it in the ancient liturgies, and it should have richer meaning for us in the
context of the Mass—and especially in the context of the
Mass as heaven on earth. We have renewed our baptism
as children of God, Whom we can call "Our Father." We
are now in heaven with Him, having lifted up our hearts.
We have hallowed His name by praying the Mass. By unit-
ing our sacrifice with Jesus' eternal sacrifice, we have seen
God's will done "on earth as it is in heaven." We have
before us Jesus, our "daily bread," and this bread will
"forgive us our trespasses," because Holy Communion
wipes away all venial sins. We have known mercy, then,
and so we will show mercy, forgiving "those who trespass
against us." And through Holy Communion we will know
new strength over temptations and evil. The Mass fulfills
the Lord's Prayer, perfectly, word for word.

[handwritten margin: arrgh! · that's what concerns me here]

We can't overemphasize the relationship between
"our daily bread" and the Eucharistic host before us. In
his classic essay on the Our Father, Scripture scholar Father Raymond Brown demonstrated that this was the
overwhelming belief of the early Christians: "There is
good reason, then, for connecting the Old Testament
manna and the New Testament Eucharistic bread with
the petition . . . Thus, in asking the Father 'Give us our

bread,' the community was employing words directly connected with the Eucharist. And so our Roman Liturgy
may not be too far from the original sense of the petition
in having the [Our Father] introduce the Communion of
the Mass."

So the "Communion Rite" begins, and we shouldn't
miss the original power of the word *communion*. In Jesus'
time, the word (in Greek, *koinonia*) was used most often
to describe a family bond. With Communion, we renew
our bond with the eternal family, the Family Who is God,
and with God's family on earth, the Church. We express
our communion with the Church in the Sign of Peace. In
this ancient gesture, we fulfill Jesus' command that we
make peace with our neighbor before we approach the
altar (see Mt 5:24).

cool →

Our next prayer, the "Lamb of God," recalls the
Passover sacrifice and the "mercy" and "peace" of the
new Passover. The priest, then, breaks the host and lifts it
up—a Lamb "standing, as if slain" (Rev 5:6)—and calls
out the words of John the Baptist: "This is the Lamb of
God" (see Jn 1:36). And we can only respond in the
words of the Roman centurion: "Lord, I am not worthy to
receive You, but only say the word . . ." (Mt 8:8).

Then we receive Him in Holy Communion. We receive *Him*, Whom we praised in the Gloria and proclaimed in the creed! We receive *Him*, before Whom we
swore our solemn oath! We receive *Him*, Who is the New
Covenant awaited through all of human history! When
Christ comes at the end of time, He will not have one
drop more glory than He has at this moment, when we
consume *all of Him!* In the Eucharist we receive what we

will *be* for all eternity, when we are taken up to heaven to join with the heavenly throng in the marriage supper of the Lamb. At Holy Communion, we are already there. This is not a metaphor. This is the cold, calculated, precise, metaphysical truth that was taught by Jesus Christ.

I dunno . . .

YOU'RE HEAVEN-SENT

After so much that's so heavy duty, the Mass seems to end too abruptly—with a blessing and "The Mass is ended. Go in peace." It seems strange that the word "Mass" should come from these hasty final words: *Ite, missa est* (literally, "Go, it is sent"). But the ancients understood that the Mass was a sending-forth. That last line is not so much a dis*miss*al as a com*miss*ioning. We have united ourselves to Christ's sacrifice. We leave Mass now in order to live the mystery, the sacrifice, we have just celebrated, through the splendor of ordinary life in the home and in the world.

PART TWO

The Revelation of Heaven

ONE

"I Turned to See"

THE SENSE AMID
THE STRANGENESS

T HOSE FIRST FOUR CHAPTERS were the easier
part. Most Catholics, after all, have at least a glanc-
ing awareness of the Mass. They're familiar with the
prayers and gestures, even if they've only endured them
sleepily. With this chapter, however, we turn to see (Rev
1:12) what many Catholics have turned away from—
sometimes in terror, sometimes in frustration.

The Book of Revelation, the last book in the Bible,
seems a weird book indeed: full of frightening wars and
consuming fires, rivers of blood, and streets paved with
gold. In all of its parts, the book seems to defy common
sense and good taste. Let's take just one famous example,
the plague of locusts. John reports that "from the smoke
came locusts . . . like horses arrayed for battle; on their
heads were what looked like crowns of gold; their faces
were like human faces, their hair like women's hair, and

[61]

their teeth like lions' teeth; they had scales like iron breastplates, and the noise of their wings was like the noise of many chariots. . . . They have tails like scorpions, and stings, and their power of hurting men for five months lies in their tails" (Rev 9:3, 7–10).

We hardly know whether to laugh or scream with fright. With all due respect, we want to ask St. John, "Okay, let me get this straight: you saw long-haired locusts with lion's teeth and human faces . . . and they were wearing golden crowns and armor?" The great temptation is just to excuse ourselves from reading the Apocalypse, reminding God that we have pressing appointments here on earth.

I am not going to deny that the details of the Book of Revelation are exceedingly strange. Instead, I'll invite you to come with me on an investigation, so that you can discover, as I did, that there is sense amid the strangeness.

THE BLOT WITH NO PLOT?

When I started my study of the Book of Revelation, I was a Protestant, evangelical in expression, Calvinist in theology. Like many other evangelicals, I found the Apocalypse fascinating. It is Scripture, of course, and I held "Scripture alone" to be the rule of faith. What's more, Revelation holds a conspicuous position as the *final book* of the Bible—God's "last word," as it were. Also, Revelation seemed to me the most mysterious and cryptic book of the Bible, and I found that just too tantalizing to pass up. I saw the Apocalypse as a puzzle that God dared me to solve, a code that begged to be cracked.

I had a lot of company. As the second millennium drew to its close, interpretation of the Book of Revelation exploded into a cottage industry among my evangelical brethren. With every trip to the bookstore, I discovered new and more promising revelations of Revelation.

This was not always the case with Protestant interpreters. The very first Protestant, Martin Luther, found the Apocalypse entirely too bizarre. For a while, he even rejected its place in the Bible, because, he said, "a revelation should be revealing." Yet Revelation *is* always revealing, in that it unmasks the prejudices, anxieties, and ideological bent of each particular interpreter.

The Apocalypse remains a sort of Rorschach blot for Christians. Preachers try first to discern an order in the text. This is usually a fruitless effort, since the book lacks the ordering principles of a literary work: a conventional story line or an argument. Failing to find order, they try to impose order. This is, more or less, the pattern I followed during my years as a Protestant seminarian and minister. What usually happens is that a particular detail seizes the imagination and becomes the interpretive key for reading the entire book. The "millennium," for example—a concept that appears only in chapter 20 of the Apocalypse—begins to color everything one sees in chapters 1–19, and 21–22.

MILLENNIUM BUG

The millennium is, today, the favored interpretive key among evangelicals and fundamentalists. Hal Lindsey's 1970 blockbuster, *The Late, Great Planet Earth,* launched a genre, as it became the second-biggest-selling book of the last thirty years. Its sales have, at last count, exceeded 35 million copies in fifty languages. Lindsey contended that the prophecies of Revelation were a precise forecast of future events, a future that was just dawning in the 1970s. He saw Revelation's strange imagery as corresponding exactly to people, places, and events that were then in the news. Russia was the beast, for example; and Gog and Magog applied to the Soviet Union. Lindsey predicted that the Soviets would swoop down upon Palestine; but Jesus would return and slaughter them and establish a thousand-year kingdom in Jerusalem.

Lindsey was not alone. In fact, for a few years, I was firmly with him—though with shades of difference—in the "futurist" camp of Revelation's interpreters. Within this camp, there is much disagreement over when the events will take place, and which of Revelation's beasts will correspond with which world leaders. Futurists also disagree among themselves as to whether Christians will go through the "tribulation," and when the world will eventually enter Christ's thousand-year reign. Some have developed new concepts such as the "Rapture" to describe the miraculous interventions they predict for the end times. At the Rapture, they say, God will sweep His chosen ones into the clouds to live with Him (see 1 Thess 4:16–17).

I ranged in these pastures for years, but without finding any real satisfaction. What happened again and again was that a preacher would fixate on a single element—the number of the beast, for instance—and his whole reading of Revelation would hinge on the identification of that number with someone in the news. Yet, through the 1970s and 1980s, world leaders rose and fell, and empires crumbled, and with every fallen leader, and with every crumbling empire, I watched another grand theory collapse into ruin.

Gradually, I began to see a larger reason for my disillusion. Would God really have inspired John's Apocalypse just so that it could sit dormant in the back of the Bible, strange and inexplicable, for twenty centuries—until the time was fulfilled and the cataclysms came to pass? No, Revelation was intended to *reveal,* and its revelations must be for all Christians of all time, including its original readers in the first century.

A BLAST FROM THE PAST

The futurists, varied as they were, did not exhaust the interpretive perspectives on the Book of Revelation. Some (called "idealists") thought the whole book was merely a metaphor for the struggles of the spiritual life. Others thought the Apocalypse outlined a plan for the history of the Church. Still others argued that the book was simply an encoded description of the first-century Christians' political situation. The thrust of the Apocalypse, according to this view, was to exhort believers to remain steadfast in the faith, and to promise divine vengeance against the Church's persecutors. I found some value in these arguments, especially as they related to some specific verses, but none was able to satisfy my desire to comprehend the unfolding of John's narrative.

The more I studied the commentaries on Revelation, the more I came to understand selected details, but the less I seemed to understand the whole of the book. Then, while researching other matters, I happened upon a hidden treasure—hidden, that is, from someone studying the Scriptures in a tradition that reaches back only four hundred years.

I began reading the Church Fathers, the Christian writers and teachers of the first eight centuries, and especially their commentaries on the Bible. I kept bumping up against my ignorance as the Fathers frequently referred to something I knew nothing about: the liturgy. Interestingly, however, I discovered that this ancient liturgy seemed to incorporate many of the small details of the Apocalypse—in a context in which they made sense! Then, as I pressed on to read the Fathers' exegetical studies of the Apocalypse, I found that many of these men had made the explicit connection between the Mass and the Book of Revelation. In fact, for most of the early Christians it was a given: the Book of Revelation was incomprehensible apart from the liturgy.

As I described in chapter 1, it was only when I began attending Mass that the many parts of this puzzling book suddenly began to fall into place. Before long, I could *see* the sense in Revelation's altar (Rev 8:3), its robed clergymen (4:4), candles (1:12), incense (5:8), manna (2:17), chalices (ch. 16), Sunday worship (1:10), the prominence it gives to the Blessed Virgin Mary (12:1–6), the "Holy, Holy, Holy" (4:8), the Gloria (15:3–4), the Sign of the Cross (14:1), the Alleluia (19:1, 3, 6), the readings from Scripture (ch. 2–3), and the "Lamb of God" (many, many times). These are not interruptions in the narrative or incidental details; they are the very stuff of the Apocalypse.

WHYS-ING UP

So Revelation wasn't just a veiled warning about 1970s geopolitics, or an encoded history of the first-century Roman Empire, or an instruction book for the end times. It was, somehow, about the very sacrament that was beginning to draw this "Bible Christian" into the fullness of Catholic faith.

Yet new questions arose. If, in the texts of the ancient liturgies, I had stumbled upon the "what" of Revelation, I was left with some whopping "whys." Why such an odd presentation? Why a vision and not a liturgical text? Why was Revelation attributed to John, of all possible disciples? Why was it written when it was written?

The answers emerged as I began to study the times of the Apocalypse and the liturgy of the times.

HEAVEN AND EARTH IN MINIATURE

Many small details of John's vision become clear when we try to encounter the book as its original audience might have. If we were Greek-speaking Jewish Christians of John's time, living in the cities of the Roman province of

Asia, we would probably know Jerusalem's topography from our regular pilgrimages. Jerusalem was supremely important for John's readers. It was the capital city and economic center of ancient Israel, as well as the nation's cultural and academic hub. But, above all, Jerusalem was the spiritual heart of the Israelite people. Try to imagine a modern city that would combine Washington, D.C., Wall Street, Oxford, and the Vatican. That's Jerusalem to a first-century Jew.

Within Jerusalem, we would feel our deepest affection for the Temple, which was the center of religious and cultural life for Jews throughout the world. Jerusalem wasn't so much a city with a Temple as a Temple with a city built around it. More than a place of worship, the Temple stood, for pious Jews, as a scale model of all creation. Just as the universe was made to be God's sanctuary, with Adam serving as priest, so the Temple was to restore this order, with the priests of Israel ministering before the Holy of Holies.

As Jewish Christians, we would immediately recognize the Temple in Revelation's description of heaven. In the Temple, as in John's heaven, the Menorah (seven golden lamp stands, Rev 1:12) and the altar of incense (8:3–5) stood before the Holy of Holies. In the Temple, four carved cherubim adorned the walls, as the four living creatures minister before the throne in John's heaven. Revelation 4:4's twenty-four "elders" (in Greek, *presbyteroi,* whence the English "priest") replicate the twenty-four priestly divisions who served in the Temple in any given year. The "sea of glass like crystal" (Rev 4:6) was the Temple's large pool of polished bronze that held

11,500 gallons of water. At the center of Revelation's Temple, as in Solomon's Temple, was the Ark of the Covenant (Rev 11:19).

Revelation revealed the Temple—but, to devout Jews and Jewish converts to Christianity, it also revealed much more. For the Temple and its trappings pointed to higher realities. Like Moses (see Ex 25:9), King David had received the plan of the Temple from God Himself: "All this he made clear by the writing from the hand of the Lord concerning it, all the work to be done according to the plan" (1 Chr 28:19). The Temple was to be modeled after the court of heaven: "You have given command to build a Temple on Your holy mountain, and an altar in the city of Your habitation, a copy of the holy tent which You prepared from the beginning" (Wis 9:8).

FROM IMITATION TO PARTICIPATION

According to ancient Jewish beliefs, the worship in Jerusalem's Temple mirrored the worship of the angels in heaven. The levitical priesthood, the covenant liturgy, the sacrifices served as shadowy representations of heavenly models.

Still, the Book of Revelation was up to something different, something more. Whereas Israel prayed *in imitation of the angels,* the Church of the Apocalypse worshiped *together with the angels* (see 19:10). Whereas only the priests were allowed in the holy place of Jerusalem's Temple, Revelation showed a nation of priests (see 5:10; 20:6) dwelling always in the presence of God.

No longer would there be a heavenly archetype and

an earthly imitation. Revelation now revealed *one worship*, shared by men and angels!

OUT OF THE ASHES

Scholars disagree on when the Book of Revelation was written; estimates range from the late 60s to the late 90s A.D. Almost all agree, however, that John's measurement of the Temple (Rev 11:1) points to a pre-70 date, since after 70 there would have been no Temple to measure.

In any case, the sacrificial worship of the Old Covenant met its definitive end with the destruction of the Temple and the leveling of Jerusalem in A.D. 70. To Jews throughout the world, this was a cataclysmic event— prefiguring the final judgment of the "cosmic temple" at the end of time. After A.D. 70, no longer would smoke rise from the lambs of Israel's sacrifices. The Roman legions had reduced to charred rubble the city and the sanctuary that had given meaning to the lives of Jews in Palestine and abroad.

What John describes in his vision was nothing less than the passing away of the old world, the old Jerusalem, the Old Covenant, and the creation of a new world, a new Jerusalem, a New Covenant. With the new world order came a new order of worship.

It's hard *not* to hear echoes from John's Gospel: "Destroy this Temple, and in three days I will raise it up" (Jn 2:19). "The hour is coming when neither on this mountain nor in Jerusalem will you worship the Father . . . when the true worshipers will worship the Father in spirit and truth" (Jn 4:21, 23). In the Apocalypse, these predictions are fulfilled, as the new Temple is revealed to be Christ's mystical body, the Church, and as worship "in the Spirit" takes place in the new and heavenly Jerusalem.

Likewise, it's easy to understand why the early Christians considered the torn Temple veil so theologically and liturgically significant. The veil was torn just as Christ's body was decisively torn. As Jesus completed the earthly offering of His body, God made sure that the world would know that the veil had been removed from "the Temple." Now everyone—brought together in the Church—could enter His presence on the Lord's Day.

> Therefore, brethren, since we have confidence to enter the sanctuary by the blood of Jesus, by the new and living way which He opened for us through the curtain [or veil], that is, through His flesh . . . let us consider how to stir up one another to love and good works, not neglecting to meet together . . . but encouraging one another, and all the more as you see the Day drawing near (Heb 10:19–20, 24–25).

"In the Spirit on the Lord's day," John saw something that was more sweeping than any narrative or any argument could convey. He saw that part of the world was already taken up into a new heaven and a new earth.

Some centuries later, I, too, began to turn and see.

TWO

Who's Who in Heaven

REVELATION'S CAST
OF THOUSANDS

EXCEPT FOR A PLAGUE of antichrist flicks in the 1970s, Hollywood hasn't even tried to screen an Apocalypse, as it has the Gospels and the Book of Exodus. Perhaps some things are just too strange, bloody, violent, and extravagant, even for Hollywood.

Or maybe directors are put off by the casting that Revelation would demand (not to mention the cost of special effects!). Cecil B. DeMille could content himself with a cast of thousands in *The Ten Commandments*. Revelation, though, would require literally *hundreds of thousands*. It is perhaps the most populous book of the Bible.

Who are these characters that fill the landscapes and heavenscapes of John? In this chapter, we'll try to get to know them a little better.

But first, a confession: I fear to tread here. Perhaps no subject more fascinates or obsesses Revelation scholars, preachers, and hobbyists than the identification of the book's beasts, critters, angels, and people.

A reader's identification of these characters depends largely on his scheme of interpretation. The futurist scheme has inspired interpreters to identify the beasts, in turn, with Napoleon, Bismarck, Hitler, and Stalin, among others. The "preterist" view—which emphasizes a first-century fulfillment of Revelation's prophecies—tends to identify the beasts, for example, with one or another Roman Emperor, or with Rome itself, or with Jerusalem. A third perspective, sometimes called the "idealist," sees Revelation as an allegory of the spiritual warfare that every believer must fight. Yet another view, the "historicist," holds that the Apocalypse lays out God's master plan for history, from beginning to end.

Which view do I follow? Well, all of them. There's no reason they can't all be true simultaneously. Scripture's riches are boundless. The earliest Christians taught that the sacred text operates on four levels, and all of those levels, all at once, teach God's one truth—like a symphony. If I favor one perspective over the others, it is the preterist. Yet, again, I won't discount the others. What binds them all together is what binds us all to Christ: the New Covenant, sealed and renewed by the Eucharistic liturgy.

For within the Apocalypse emerges a pattern—of covenant, fall, judgment, and redemption—and this pattern does describe a particular period of history, but it also describes *every* period of history, and *all* of history, as well as the course of life for each and every one of us.

"I, JOHN"

I mentioned earlier that there is much controversy over John's authorship of the Book of Revelation. That debate, while fascinating, is only incidental to our study of the Mass and the Apocalypse.

One thing, however, is clear: the text explicitly associates itself with John (Rev 1:4, 9; 22:8). And "John" in the New Testament (and in the minds of the early Church Fathers) means John the Apostle.

Indeed, the books themselves indicate that, if they do not share a common author, they at least flow from the same school of thought. For Revelation and the Fourth Gospel share many theological concerns. Both books reveal a rather precise knowledge of the Jerusalem Temple and its rituals; both seem preoccupied with presenting Jesus as the "Lamb," the sacrifice of the new Passover (see Jn 1:29, 36; Rev 5:6). Moreover, John's Gospel and the Apocalypse share some terminology that, within the New Testament, is peculiar only to them. For example, only the Fourth Gospel and the Apocalypse refer to Jesus as "the Word of God" (Jn 1:1; Rev 19:13); and only these two books refer to New Covenant worship as "in the Spirit" (Jn 4:23; Rev 1:10). Also, only these two books speak of salvation in terms of "living water" (Jn 4:13; Rev 21:6). There are many other parallels as well.

Still, this identification of the author John with the Apostle John is important only because of the insight it gives us into the power of Revelation's vision. In the Gospel, for example, John is identified as the "Beloved Disci-

ple" of Jesus (see Jn 13:23; 21:20, 24). John was the
Apostle on most intimate terms with the Lord, the disciple who was literally closest to His heart. John reclined on
Jesus' breast at the Last Supper. Yet, in the Apocalypse,
when he saw Jesus in His power and glory, with universal
dominion and divine sovereignty, John fell on his face
(see Rev 1:17). These are important details for us, who
want to be "beloved disciples" today. While we must
strive for an increasingly intimate relationship with Jesus,
we can hardly begin the conversation until we see Jesus
for Who He is, in His all-surpassing holiness.

John's identity is important also in relation to Revelation's earthly concerns. Tradition identifies the Apostle
John as bishop of Ephesus, one of the seven churches
addressed in Revelation. The churches are identified with
cities, all seven of which were located within a fifty-mile
radius in Asia Minor, probably marking off the sphere of
John's authority. We can see why John, as bishop, would
be chosen to deliver such a pastoral message as we find in
Revelation, especially in the letters to the seven churches
(Rev 2, 3).

"THE LAMB"

This is Revelation's favored title and image for Jesus
Christ. Yes, He is ruler (1:5); He stands amid the Meno-
rah robed as high priest (1:13); He is "the first and the
last" (1:17), "the holy one" (3:7), "Lord of lords and
King of kings" (17:14)—but, overwhelmingly, Jesus is the
Lamb.

The Lamb, according to the *Catechism of the Catholic*

Church, is "Christ crucified and risen, the one high priest of the true sanctuary, the same one 'Who offers and is offered, Who gives and is given' " (no. 1137).

When John first sees the Lamb, he's actually looking for a lion. No one is able to open the seals of the scroll and reveal its contents, and John begins to weep. Then an elder reassures him, "Weep not; lo, the Lion of the tribe of Judah, the Root of David, has conquered, so that He can open the scroll and its seven seals" (Rev 5:5).

John looks around for the Lion of Judah, but instead sees—a Lamb. Lambs are not very mighty to begin with, and this one is standing "as though it had been slain" (Rev 5:6). We don't need to revisit here all that we discussed in chapter 2. What should be clear is that Jesus, here, is a sacrificial lamb, like the Passover lamb.

The elders *(presbyteroi,* priests) then sing that Christ's sacrifice has enabled Him to break the seals of the scroll, the Old Testament. "Worthy are You to take the scroll and to open its seals, for You were slain, and by Your blood You ransomed men for God" (5:9). Heaven and earth then give glory to Jesus as to God: "To Him Who sits upon the throne and to the Lamb be blessing and honor and glory and might for ever and ever! . . . and the elders fell down and worshiped" (5:13–14).

The Lamb is Jesus. The Lamb is also a "son of man," robed as a high priest (1:13); the Lamb is sacrificial victim; the Lamb is God.

"A WOMAN CLOTHED WITH THE SUN"

Revelation 12, John's vision of the woman clothed with the sun, captures the essence of the Book of Revelation. With many layers of meaning, it shows a past event prefiguring an event far off in the future. It recaps the Old Testament as it completes the New. It reveals heaven, but in images of earth.

John's vision begins with the opening of God's temple in heaven, "and the ark of His covenant was seen within the temple" (Rev 11:19). Perhaps we can't fully appreciate the shock value of that line. The Ark of the Covenant had not been seen for five centuries. At the time of the Babylonian captivity, the prophet Jeremiah had hidden the ark in a place that "shall be unknown until God gathers His people together again" (2 Mac 2:7).

That promise is fulfilled in John's vision. The Temple appeared, "and there were flashes of lightning, loud noises, peals of thunder, an earthquake, and heavy hail." And then: "A great portent appeared in heaven, a woman clothed with the sun, with the moon under her feet, and on her head a crown of twelve stars; she was with child" (Rev 12:1–2).

John would not have introduced the ark, just to drop it immediately. I believe (with the Fathers of the Church) that when John describes the woman, he is describing the ark—of the New Covenant. And who is the woman? She is the one who gives birth to the male child Who will rule the nations. The child is Jesus; His mother is Mary.

[77]

What made the original ark so holy? Not the gold that coated the outside, but the Ten Commandments inside—the Law that had been inscribed by the finger of God on tablets of stone. What else was inside? Manna, the miracle bread that fed the people in their pilgrimage through the wasteland; Aaron's rod that blossomed as a sign of his office as high priest (see Nm 17).

What makes the new ark holy? The old ark contained the word of God written in stone; Mary contained in her womb the Word of God Who became man and dwelt among us. The ark contained manna; Mary contained the living bread come down from heaven. The ark contained the rod of the high priest Aaron; Mary's womb contained the eternal high priest, Jesus Christ. In the heavenly temple, the Word of God is Jesus, and the ark in whom he resides is Mary, His mother.

If the male child is Jesus, then the woman is Mary. This interpretation was upheld by the most sober-minded of the Church Fathers, St. Athanasius, St. Epiphanius, and many others. Yet "the woman" also stands for more. She is "daughter Zion," which brought forth Israel's Messiah. She is also the Church, besieged by Satan, yet preserved in safety. As I said before, Scripture's riches are boundless.

Other scholars argue that the woman cannot be Mary, since, according to Catholic tradition, Mary suffered no labor pain. The pangs of the woman, however, need not have been physical pain. St. Paul, for example, used birth pangs to describe his own agony until Christ be formed in his disciples (see Gal 4:19). Thus, the suffering of the woman could describe the suffering of a soul—the suffering that Mary knew, at the foot of the cross, as she became the mother of all "beloved disciples" (see Jn 19:25–27).

Others object that the woman cannot be Mary because the woman in Revelation has other offspring, and the Church teaches that Mary was perpetually virgin. But Scripture often uses the term "offspring" (in Greek, *sperma)* to describe one's spiritual descendants. The children of Mary, her spiritual offspring, are those "who keep the commandments of God and bear testimony to Jesus" (Rev 12:17). We are the other offspring of the woman. We are the children of Mary.

Thus, Revelation also portrays Mary as the "New Eve," mother of all the living. In the Garden of Eden, God promised to "put enmity" between Satan, the ancient serpent, and Eve—and between Satan's "seed and her seed" (Gen 3:15). Now, in the Apocalypse, we see the climax of this enmity. The seed of the new woman, Mary, is the male son, Jesus Christ, Who comes to defeat the serpent (in Hebrew, the same word, *nahash,* can apply to both dragon and serpent).

This is the overwhelming teaching of the Fathers, Doctors, saints, and popes of the Church, both ancient and modern. It is the teaching of the *Catechism of the Catholic Church* (see no. 1138). I must point out, however, that it is not held by many biblical scholars today. Yet those who disagree must bear the burden of proof. Pope St. Pius X spoke eloquently for the Tradition in his encyclical letter *Ad Diem Illum Laetissimum:*

Everyone knows that this woman signified the Virgin Mary. . . . John therefore saw the Most Holy Mother of God already in eternal happiness, yet travailing in a mysterious childbirth. What birth was it? Surely it was the birth of us who, still in exile, are yet to be generated to the perfect charity of God, and to eternal happiness.

THE FIRST BEAST

Unsuccessful in his assaults on the woman and her son, the dragon turns to attack her offspring, on those who keep the commandments of God and bear testimony to Jesus. The dragon summons his own seed, two dreadful beasts. Oddly enough, amid all the hopeful and awe-inspiring images of the Apocalypse, these hideous monsters seem to spark the most interest. Moviemakers and televangelists dwell longer, by far, on 666 than on the glassy sea or the Lion of Judah.

I feel an urgency to impress upon you the reality of the beasts. They are symbols, but they're not *just* symbols. They are real spiritual beings, members of the satanic "lowerarchy," demonic persons who have controlled and corrupted the political destiny of nations. John describes two ugly beasts. But I believe the beasts he saw were much more horrible than his description.

In much of Revelation—but especially chapters 4 and 5—John describes the realities behind the Mass. Now, he does the same with sin and evil. Just as our actions in the liturgy are united with unseen heavenly things, so are our sinful deeds attached to infernal wickedness. In the Mass, what does God want to make us? A kingdom of priests who reign through their sacrificial offerings. On the other hand, what does Satan want to accomplish through the beasts? He wants to subvert God's plan by corrupting both kingdom and priesthood. Thus, John shows us, first, the demon that corrupts government authority, the state. Next, he reveals the demon of corrupt religious authority.

First beasts first: from the sea arises a hideous seven-headed, ten-horned monster, a terrifying combination of leopard, lion, and bear. The horns symbolize power; the diadems (or crowns), kingship. Both its power and its kingship it receives from the dragon. We would err, however, if we identified this beast with monarchy in general. No, the beast represents corrupt political authority of any sort.

It's tempting, too, to identify the beast exclusively with Rome, or with the Herodian dynasty that Rome maintained in the Holy Land. Certainly the Rome of John's day typified the sort of government represented by the beast. But the beast itself does not allow for such a simple identification. It's actually a combination of all four of the beasts from a vision of the Old Testament prophet Daniel (see Dan 7). I follow the Church Fathers, who saw Daniel's beasts pointing to four gentile empires: Babylon, Medo-Persia, Greece, and Rome—all of whom persecuted God's people before the Messiah's coming.

Revelation's seven-headed beast, then, stands for all corrupted political power. For it's a human impulse to look upon the power of the state as the greatest power on earth and say, like the people in the Apocalypse, "Who can fight against it?" Out of fear for this power—or desire for a piece of the action—people constantly compromise themselves and worship the dragon and the beast. History's most blatant example of a human institution usurping God's prerogatives is Rome and its Caesars. They literally demanded the worship that belongs to God alone. And they made war on the saints, instigating bloody persecutions of those who would not worship the emperor.

Again, however, I must emphasize that the beast is not only Rome, or only Rome's puppet, the Herodians. The beast refers also to any corrupt government, any state that puts itself above God's covenant order. More than that, the beast represents the corrupting spiritual force behind these institutions.

THE SECOND BEAST

This beast comes from the earth and has horns like a lamb. The lamb imagery is jarring, as we've come by now to associate it with sacred things. John's use of it, I believe, is intentional, for I believe that this beast is meant to suggest the corrupted priesthood in first-century Jerusalem.

The initial clue is that this beast comes out of "the earth," which in the original Greek could also mean "the land" or "the country," as opposed to "the sea," which brings forth the gentile beasts (see Dan 7). Further, John was likely bearing witness to the ultimate compromise of priestly authority, which had occurred only a few years before. In a dramatic historical moment, religious authority had given its allegiance to corrupt government authority instead of God. Jesus, the Lamb of God, High King and High Priest, stood before Pontius Pilate and the chief priests of the Jews. Pilate said to the Jews, "Here is your king!" They cried out, "Away with Him, away with Him, crucify Him!" Pilate replied, "Shall I crucify your king?" The chief priests answered, "We have no king but Caesar" (see Jn 19:15). Indeed it was the high priest himself, Caiaphas, who first spoke of Jesus' sacrifice as politically "expedient" for the people (see Jn 11:47–52).

So they rejected Christ and elevated Caesar. They rejected the Lamb and worshiped the beast. Certainly Caesar was the government's ruler and as such deserved respect (see Lk 20:21–25). But Caesar wanted more than respect. He demanded sacrificial worship, which the chief priests gave him when they handed over the Lamb of God.

The beast resembles a lamb in some superficial features. We see that everything he does is in mimicry and mockery of the Lamb's saving work. The Lamb stands as though it had been slain; the beast receives a mortal wound, but recovers. God enthrones the Lamb; the dragon enthrones the beast. Those who worship the Lamb receive His sign on their foreheads (Rev 7:2–4); those who worship the beast wear the mark of the beast.

Which brings us to the difficult question: What is the mark of the beast? John tells us that it is the name of the beast, or the number of its name. What is that? John answers in a riddle: "This calls for wisdom: let him who has understanding reckon the number of the beast, for it is a human number, its number is six hundred and sixty-six" (Rev 13:18).

On one level, the number may represent the Roman emperor Nero, whose name transliterated into Hebrew indeed has the value 666. Yet there are many other, or additional, possibilities. Consider that 666 was the number of gold talents King Solomon required from the nations yearly (see 1 Kgs 10). Consider also that Solomon was the first priest-king since Melchizedek (see Ps 110). Moreover, John says that discerning the identity of the beast "calls for wisdom," which some interpreters have seen as another reference to Solomon, who was renowned for his wisdom.

Finally, 666 can be interpreted as a degradation of the number seven, which, in Israel's tradition, represented perfection, holiness, and the covenant. The seventh day, for example, was declared holy by God and set aside for rest and worship. Work was done in six days; it was sanctified, however, in the sacrificial worship represented by the seventh day. The number "666," then, represents a man stalled in the sixth day, serving the beast who concerns himself with buying and selling (see Rev 13:17) without rest for worship. Though work is holy, it becomes evil when man refuses to offer it to God.

Yet we must be clear about something. This interpretation should not lead any Christian to justify anti-Semitism. The Book of Revelation overwhelmingly demonstrates the dignity of Israel—its Temple, its prophets, its covenants. The Apocalypse should rather lead us to a greater appreciation for our heritage in Israel—and to a sober consideration of our own accountability before God. How well are we living according to *our* covenant with God? How faithful are we to *our* priesthood? The book stands as a warning to all of us.

The beastly message is this: we are fighting spiritual forces: immense, depraved, malevolent forces. If we had to fight them alone, we'd be trounced. But here's good news: there is a way we can hope to overcome. The solution has to match the problem, spiritual force for spiritual force, immense beauty for immense ugliness, holiness for depravity, love for malevolence. The solution is the Mass, when heaven touches down to save an earth under siege.

ANGELS

In battle, we do not fight alone. In Revelation 12, we read of "Michael and his angels fighting against the dragon" (12:7).

When God created the angels, He made them free, and so they had to undergo some sort of test—just as our life on earth is a test. No one knows what this test was, but some theologians speculate that the angels were given a vision of the Incarnation, and they were told they would have to serve the incarnate deity, Jesus, and His mother. Satan's pride revolted against the scandal of Spirit taking on the bonds of matter, and he said, "I will not serve!" According to the Church Fathers, he led one third of the angels in this rebellion (see Rev 12:4). Michael and his angels cast them out of heaven (see v. 8).

Throughout the Apocalypse, we see that the angels populate heaven rather densely. They worship God without ceasing (Rev 4:8). And they watch over us. Chapters 2 and 3 make clear that each particular church has a guardian angel. This should reassure us, who belong to particular churches, and who can call for help from our particular church's angel.

The "four living creatures" mentioned in chapter 4 are usually understood to be angels, though they appear to human eyes in animal form. These creatures may correspond as well to the creatures embroidered on the screen before the Holy of Holies in Jerusalem's Temple.

Though heaven's angels present themselves to human eyes in physical form, angels do not actually have bodies. Their name means "messenger," and the physical attributes usually symbolize some aspect of their nature or mission. Wings indicate their swiftness in moving between heaven and earth. Multiple eyes signify their knowledge and watchfulness. Many-eyed, six-winged angels might sound scary at first, but if we think of them in terms of their swiftness and vigilance, we'll be reassured. These are beings we can count on, when the dragon threatens our peace.

In Revelation, the angels also appear as horsemen (ch. 6) who visit God's judgment upon unfaithful people (see also Zec 1:7–17). Much of the action in these chapters may be connected to the events surrounding the fall of Jerusalem in A.D. 70. But the passage has applications beyond the first century, as long as the earth stands in need of judgment.

Revelation's angels control the elements, the wind and sea, to do God's will (ch. 7). Chapters 7–9 make it clear that angels are mighty warriors, and that they battle constantly on the side of God—which, if we're faithful, is our side, too.

MARTYRS, VIRGINS, AND OTHER FOLKS

But there's more to the Apocalypse than wicked beasts and awesome angels. In fact, most of the characters are just plain folks—hundreds of thousands, and even millions, are ordinary Christian men and women. First, we see the 144,000 from the twelve tribes of Israel (12,000 from each tribe), the remnant who received God's protection (His "sign"), fleeing to the mountains during Jerusalem's destruction. Then, John describes myriads of myriads "from every nation" (Rev 7:9). After two millennia of inclusive religion, we cannot today appreciate the seismic impact of this vision of Israelites worshiping together with gentiles, and humans with angels. To the minds of John's first readers, these were mutually exclusive categories. Moreover, in heaven, all these multitudes worship within the Holy of Holies, where none but the High Priest had previously been admitted. The New Covenant people can worship God face to face.

Who else is there? In chapter 6, we encounter the martyrs, those who had been slain for the witness of their faith. "I saw under the altar the souls of those who had been slain for the word of God and for the witness they had borne" (Rev 6:9). Why are they under the altar? What was usually under the altar of the earthly Temple? When Old Testament priests offered animal sacrifices, the victims' blood gathered under the altar. As priestly people, they (and we) offer up our lives upon the earth, the true altar, as a sacrifice to God. The true sacrifice then is not an animal; it is every saint who gives testimony (in Greek, *martyria)* to God's faithfulness. Our offering—the martyrs' blood—calls out to God for vindication. How revealing that, from the earliest days, the Church has placed the relics of the martyrs, their bones and ashes, within its altars. Earlier, we mentioned the elders *(presbyteroi)* enthroned at God's court. Indeed, in Revelation's heaven, these men appear vested exactly as Israel's priests dressed for service in Jerusalem's Temple.

In Revelation (14:4), we also encounter a large number of men consecrated to virginity. This is another anomaly in the ancient world, found rarely in Israel or gentile cultures, as it has been unusual in the Christian West ever since the Protestant Reformation. Yet John mentions these celibates as a veritable army, which is more probably what God intends (see 1 Cor 6–7).

ON EARTH AS IN HEAVEN

We don't have to go very far afield in order to identify the cast of characters in the Apocalypse. In fact, the meaning God wishes us to see is often plainly told in the text, or plainly wanting in our hearts. As I look back on my own years of studying Revelation as a Protestant, I marvel that my brethren and I could sometimes see, very clearly, Soviet helicopters portrayed in the plague of mutant locusts—yet we were vehement in denying that Mary could be the woman clothed with the sun, who gave birth to the male child Who saved the world. Reading the Apocalypse, we must always fight the temptation to strain for the extravagant while denying the obvious.

I'll say it again: Often the deepest meaning in Scripture is very near to the heart of each of us, and the widest application is very close to home.

Now, where on earth can we find a universal Church that worships in a manner that is true to John's vision? Where can we find priests in vestments standing before an altar? Where do we encounter men consecrated to celibacy? Where do we hear the angels invoked? Where do we find a Church that keeps the relics of the saints within its altars? Where does art extol the woman crowned with the stars, with the moon at her feet, who crushes the head of the serpent? Where do the faithful pray for the protection of St. Michael the archangel?

Where else but in the Catholic Church, and most particularly in the Mass?

THREE

Apocalypse Then!

THE BATTLES OF REVELATION
AND THE ULTIMATE WEAPON

THE FINAL CONFLAGRATION. *The Battle of Armageddon.* Revelation's most sensational publicity, over the last generations, has come from its images of combat. For its war is not just any war, but the ultimate war, and it is terrible indeed: "demonic spirits . . . go abroad to the kings of the whole world, to assemble them for battle" (Rev 16:14). John describes a world war that is simultaneously an otherworldly war: "Now war arose in heaven, Michael and his angels fighting against the dragon" (12:7). Angels pour out the chalices of God's wrath, and strong armies retreat in fear. Casualty counts run high, and the tribulations extend even to God's people. Darkness seems to have its day.

Futurists such as Hal Lindsey have claimed that these details correspond literally to a battle that the world is fast approaching at the turn of the millennium. In a similar vein, some Catholic futurists discern a unity of witness in the vision of John, the predictions of Fatima, and events in the news today.

I do not rule out the futurist interpretations of Revelation's battles. Perhaps all of the apocalyptic details will play themselves out, in one way or another, when God brings on the close of this age. Yet I do not believe that the futurist reading should be our primary focus when we read the Book of Revelation. The predictions, after all, may be of urgent concern to those who are living at the time of the final battle. But this we can never know for sure. Generations of futurists have gone before us, and died, wasting precious years on obsessive worries that Napoleon, Hitler, or Stalin was, at last, the beast foretold.

Beastly rulers come and go; futurist scenarios arise and dissipate like smoke rings, as last year's future fades into history. Revelation's other "senses," however, remain with us, with a constant urgency, a personal call.

CRASHING SYMBOLS

What do we mean by the senses of Scripture? From the earliest times, Christian teachers have spoken of the Bible as having a *literal sense* and a *spiritual sense*. The literal sense may describe a historical person, place, or event. The spiritual sense speaks—*through that same person, place, or event*—to reveal a truth about Jesus Christ, or the moral life, or the destiny of our souls, or all three.

Tradition teaches us, however, that the literal sense is foundational. Yet identifying the literal sense of the Book of Revelation is a most difficult enterprise, and it's bound to be controversial. After all, interpreters are sharply divided over whether the book is literally describing past events or future events—or past *and* future events, for the Apocalypse may apply quite concretely to both. St. Augustine spoke of these difficulties in his book *The City of God,* and St. Thomas Aquinas echoed his perplexity in the *Summa Theologica:* "But it is not easy to know what these signs may be: for the signs of which we read . . . refer not only to Christ's coming to judgment, but also to the time of the sack of Jerusalem, and to the coming of Christ in ceaselessly visiting His Church."

Interpreting the Book of Revelation is further complicated because the literal and spiritual senses seem to merge in John's vision. While John's Gospel is a work of subtle art, his Apocalypse applies symbols with a heavy hand. John speaks of a city, for example, and tells you that its names ("Egypt" and "Sodom") are figurative; then, with no further ado, he tells you which city it really is (see Rev 11:8). Even when he makes a riddle of a beast's name, he tells you clearly that he's making a riddle.

Now is no time to be overly subtle, John seems to say. And why is that? Because he was living in a time of war.

HOW SOON IS "SOON"?

In the Apocalypse, John alludes to the severe trials Christians faced in his day. Since he rarely names names—and he never tells you the date, except to say it was "the Lord's day"—interpreters offer a long list of candidates for Revelation's tribulations: the fall of Jerusalem and destruction of the Temple (A.D. 70); the emperor Nero's bloody persecution (A.D. 64); the later persecution by the emperor Domitian (A.D. 96); the earlier persecution of Christians by Jews (50s and 60s A.D.).

In a sense, of course—a spiritual sense—all of these interpretations are true, because Revelation does offer encouragement to all Christians who undergo trials or persecution, to any degree. But in a literal sense, Revelation is, I believe, primarily about the fall of Jerusalem.

From the very beginning, Revelation has an imminent tone: "The revelation of Jesus Christ which God gave him to show to his servants *what must soon take place*" (Rev 1:1). The message recurs throughout the book: "I am coming soon" (see 1:1, 3; 3:11; 22:6–7, 10, 12, 20). Jesus Himself indicated that He would return soon, even before a generation had passed since His resurrection. "There are some standing here who will not taste death before they see the Son of Man coming in His kingdom" (Mt 16:28). "This generation will not pass away till all these things take place" (Mt 24:34).

Today, most of us associate the "soon" with the Second Coming of Jesus at the end of the world. And this is surely true; both John and Jesus were speaking about the end of history. I think, however, that they were also—and primarily—speaking about the end of *a* world: the destruction of the Jerusalem Temple, and with it the end of the world of the Old Covenant, with its sacrifices and rituals, its barriers to gentiles, and its barriers between heaven and earth. Yet the *Parousia* (or "coming") of Jesus was to be more than an ending; it was a beginning, a *new* Jerusalem, a *New* Covenant, a *new* heaven and earth.

Both John and Jesus refer not only to a distant *Parousia*, or return—but to Jesus' ongoing *Parousia*, which did take place within the first Christian generation, as it still takes place today. We should not forget that the original meaning of the Greek *Parousia* is "presence," and Jesus' presence is real and abiding in the Blessed Sacrament of the Eucharist. So when John and Jesus said "soon," I believe they meant it quite literally. For the Church is the kingdom already begun on earth, and it is the place of the *Parousia* in every Mass.

WHORES AND RUMORS OF WAR

John clearly indicates that the "great city" of Revelation 11 is Jerusalem. He wrote: "Their dead bodies will lie in the street of the great city which is allegorically called Sodom and Egypt, where their Lord was crucified." In Revelation 17:6, the harlot, "drunk with the blood of the saints and the blood of the martyrs of Jesus," resonates with the Old Testament invectives against Jerusalem's infidelities. Ezekiel (see 16:2–63; 23:2–49), Jeremiah (2:20; 3:3), Isaiah (1:21), and others decry the city as a harlot. Then, in Revelation 20–21, we see the new Jerusalem descend from heaven as a virgin bride after the harlot city is destroyed. Notice the contrast: two cities, one a whore, the other a virgin bride. One Jerusalem replaces the other.

It was Jerusalem's authorities who crucified Jesus Christ. And Jerusalem was the main locus of persecution for Christians of the first generation (see Acts 6:8–14; 7:57–60; 8:1–3). The chief persecutors were the priests and pharisees such as Saul of Tarsus. The Acts of the Apostles describes constant persecution, in many cities outside Jerusalem; but in almost every case, the persecutions stem from Jewish opposition (see Acts 13:45; 14:2, 5, 19; 17:5–9, 13; 18:12–17; 21:27–32).

A TALE OF FOUR CITIES
(SODOM, EGYPT, JERICHO, BABYLON)

The details of the destruction described in Revelation correspond closely to the history of Jerusalem's destruction. In Revelation 17–19, John shows a city destroyed by fire; Jerusalem was entirely destroyed by fire. In chapters 8 and 9, John describes "the abyss," which, according to Jewish tradition, lay beneath the Foundation Stone of Jerusalem's Temple.

There is still further evidence that Jerusalem is the city depicted in the Apocalypse. Revelation closely tracks the Old Testament Book of Ezekiel, and Ezekiel's single outstanding message is that the curse of the covenant will come upon Jerusalem. We see this curse fulfilled in the Book of Revelation.

Jerusalem is "allegorically called Sodom and Egypt," says John. What is it that these places held in common? They were centers of opposition to the plan of God. Sodom stood in the way of God's covenant plan with Abraham; Egypt stood in the way of His covenant plan for Moses and Israel. Now, it's Jerusalem's turn to oppose God, as its leaders persecute the Apostles and the Church. Thus, Jerusalem, like Sodom and Egypt, had to fall, and Revelation portrays that fall in terms of seven plagues, which echo the plagues that God visited upon Egypt (see Rev 17).

When the city falls, we hear still more Old Testament echoes. For the great city falls from the blasts of seven trumpets blown by seven angels (Rev 8–9). This passage of Revelation closely follows the story of the fall of Jericho (see Jos 6:3–7). Both passages begin with silence, proceed to the seven trumpet blasts, and end with a shout. Jericho, too, had stood in the way of God's plan, by attempting to keep the Chosen People out of the Promised Land. In turn, Jerusalem, persecutor of Christians, had become a new Jericho, and thus it had to fall.

Much later in the Apocalypse, when the kings of the earth assemble for battle "on the great day of God the Almighty" (Rev 16:14), they assemble on the hill of Megiddo, or Armageddon. This location recalls yet another painful historical memory for Israel. Armageddon was the place where Josiah, the great Davidic king, amid his holy reform of Jerusalem, was cut down in his prime for disobeying the instruction of God's prophet (see 2 Kgs 23:28–30). Josiah's defeat at Megiddo weakened Israel's defenses and left Jerusalem vulnerable to destruction by Babylon. An ironic twist for the generation of Christians was that Jesus Christ—like Josiah, a Davidic king and reformer Who was cut down in His prime—would persevere in obedience and succeed where Josiah failed, establishing a new Jerusalem, witnessed by the fall of the old.

TIMES OF THE SIGN

Fall it did, as the Roman emperor Titus's armies laid siege to the city in the year A.D. 70. Siege brought on famine, pestilence, and strife, which we can see in the devastations wrought by the four angelic horsemen of Revelation 6, and by the seven angelic trumpeters of Revelation 8–9. In a manner less symbolic and more horrifically graphic, we can see these calamities described also in the writings of the Jewish historian Josephus, who was an eyewitness. Josephus describes Jerusalem so ravaged by famine that its mothers, mad with hunger, began to devour their own infants.

Yet, through all the strife of the Jewish War, not a single Christian perished, because the community of believers had fled to the mountains across the Jordan to a place called Pella. We read in Revelation 7:1–4, that these Christians—144,000 from the Twelve Tribes of Israel—were preserved because they were "sealed . . . upon their foreheads." This recalls the signing of God's remnant in Ezekiel (see Ez 9:2–4), where the Hebrew word for "sign" is *tau,* transliterated as the Greek letter "T." In A.D. 70, God similarly saved the remnant of Israel who were marked with *tau,* the Sign of the Cross. This "sealing" with the *tau* seems to be a reference to baptism, since the 144,000 are wearing white robes, the traditional baptismal garment; they're "washed in the Lamb's blood" (the cleansing effect of the Lamb's death); they're led by the Lamb to "springs of living water" (see Jn 3–4; 7); and the term for "sealed" was commonly ap-

[97]

plied to baptism in the early Church (see Rom 4–6; Eph 1:11–14; 2 Cor 1:22).

The Christians bore the sign and they counted on angelic allies. The Book of Revelation makes it clear that even though every believer must battle against powerful supernatural forces, no Christian ever fights alone. Till the end of time, Michael and the faithful angels fight on the side of the Church—and this, Revelation shows us, is the side that wins.

THE FIRST CHURCH OF CHRIST IN JERUSALEM

A fascinating, often neglected part of the historical record is that the first Christian church structure—standing on Mount Zion—survived the siege and the destruction. In A.D. 70, Rome's Tenth Legion stood between the Zion church and the burning sectors of Jerusalem. In A.D. 130, when Hadrian arrived to put down the second Jewish revolt, Jerusalem was still in ruins, reported St. Epiphanius, "except for a few houses and the little church of God on the spot where the disciples went to the upper room."

Of all the sacred sites in and around the holy city, why did God preserve the upper room? According to tradition, this was the place where Jesus instituted the Eucharist, and the spot where the Spirit descended on Pentecost. Thus it was the place where Christians were first nourished for the imminent famine, where they were sealed by the Spirit for safety in the coming destruction. This very church seems to have been preserved from the otherwise *total* destruction of Jerusalem.

SPIRITUAL SEMITES

Again we must face the question of whether John's Apocalypse—and even Christianity itself—is anti-Semitic or anti-Jewish. Isn't Revelation's analysis of the Jewish War exceedingly harsh? Was John just kicking the Chosen People while they were down?

Our answer to these questions must be a firm no. Anti-Semitism is spiritual stupidity and it renders the Apocalypse meaningless. For John's vision makes no sense unless Israel is the firstborn of all nations. As our eldest brother, Israel stood as an example for us.

You can see this vividly if you ever visit Rome. There stands the Arch of Titus, the monument erected to celebrate the Roman general's defeat of the Jews. Carved in the stone are scenes of battle and of soldiers carrying off the spoils of Jerusalem's destruction. There, amid the booty, is the Temple Menorah, the seven golden lamps.

The scenes on the arch correspond in a chilling way to Jesus' message in Revelation: "I will come to you and remove your lamp stand from its place, unless you repent" (Rev 2:5). Recall that Jesus Himself stands amid the lamp stands (see Rev 1:12–13); so to remove the lamp was to remove God's very presence. Yet here the Lord was not speaking to Jerusalem, but to the Church of Ephesus, whose love for Him had grown cold. He warned the Christians of Ephesus that, unless they changed their ways, they would suffer the same fate as their elder brother, Israel.

The sad truth is that Ephesus did lose its lamp, as did Smyrna, Pergamum, Thyatira, Sardis, Philadelphia, and Laodicea—every single one of the churches addressed in the Book of Revelation. In turn, each of those cities, once thriving Christian centers, suffered the loss of faith. Today, all are predominantly Muslim, and Catholics there require special permission just to celebrate the Mass.

Think about it: Ephesus was home, in turn, to the Blessed Virgin Mary, St. John, St. Paul, St. Barnabas, St. Timothy, Apollos—a veritable hall of fame of New Testament personages. Yet Ephesus lost its lamp, as Jerusalem had before and other prosperous churches would afterward.

No, Israel's defeat is no cause for celebration. It should cause us to tremble—because not only *can* it happen to Christians but it has, repeatedly, and it will likely happen again. If Israel the firstborn failed, so will we, younger siblings, whenever we grow proud and self-reliant.

Thus, I repeat, anti-Semitism and anti-Judaism are spiritually destructive and stupid. In the words of Pope Pius XI: "Spiritually, we are Semites." You cannot be a good Catholic until you've fallen in love with the religion and people of Israel.

WALK A CUBIT IN THEIR SANDALS

Still, the old Jerusalem had to give way to the new Jerusalem: a new covenant, a new creation, a new heaven and a new earth. After two thousand years, we Christians are comfortable with this notion—too comfortable, in fact.

But if we place ourselves imaginatively in the time of John's Revelation, we'll find that the very idea of Jerusalem's fall makes us anxious. Jerusalem was, after all, the holy city for the children of Israel; and most of the first Christians were Jews. They had to face up to the destruction of the Temple, the most beautiful building on earth, and the disappearance of a priesthood that stretched back more than a thousand years, established by God on Mount Sinai. Jesus Himself wept with love for Jerusalem, even as the town fathers plotted His execution. For these first Christians, the destruction of Jerusalem was cause for intense anxiety.

Yet Jerusalem and the Temple were indeed passing away before their eyes. Christians needed reassurance. They required an explanation. They were desperate for a revelation from God.

Through John, God revealed His covenant judgment upon old Jerusalem. The city had called forth wrath by its infidelity, by crucifying the Son of God and by persecuting the Church. Knowing this, Christians could see the context of their own persecution, and could understand why they must no longer look to old Jerusalem for their help and salvation.

Now they must look to the new Jerusalem, which was, before John's eyes, descending from heaven. Where was it touching down? On Mount Zion, where Jesus had eaten His last Passover and instituted the Eucharist. Mount Zion, where the Holy Spirit had descended upon the Apostles at Pentecost. Mount Zion, where Christians till A.D. 70 met to celebrate the Eucharist—and where the Lamb stood with the faithful remnant of Israel (Rev

14:1), who were sealed against the impending destruction. The new Jerusalem came to earth, then as now, in the place where Christians celebrated the supper of the Lamb.

THE KILLER LAMB

In the Mass, the early Christians would find strength amid persecution. From the one perpetual sacrifice of Jesus Christ would come the Church's help and salvation. The Mass is where Christians joined forces with the angels and saints to worship God, as the Book of Revelation shows us. The Mass is where the Church received "hidden manna" for sustenance in times of trial (see Rev 2:17). The Mass is where the prayers of the saints on earth rose like incense to join the prayers of angels in heaven—*and it is these prayers that altered the course of battles and the course of history.* That's the battle plan of the Apocalypse. That's how Christianity prevailed over seemingly unbeatable enemies, in Jerusalem and in Rome.

Even after Jerusalem's fall, other adversaries would rise to persecute the Church of God. In every age, the Church faces mighty persecutors, with ever more powerful armies and armaments. Yet weapons and legions and strategies all will fail. Great generals will, ultimately, fall to mortal wounds. But when the Lamb enters the fray, "Then the kings of the earth and the great men and the generals and the rich and the strong, and every one, slave and free, hid in the caves and among the rocks of the mountains, calling to the mountains and rocks, 'Fall on us and hide us from the face of Him Who is seated on the throne, and from the wrath of the Lamb; for the great day of their wrath has come, and who can stand it?' " (Rev 6:15–17).

The Church is the army of the Lamb, the forces of Zion preserved upon Jerusalem's destruction. The army of the Lamb draws strength from the banquet of heaven.

FOUR

Judgment Day

HIS MERCY IS SCARY

ECENT GENERATIONS of interpreters have fix-
ated on Revelation's wars and beasts, which are fascinating because they're frightening. Readers have
legitimate fears about how such severe judgment might
apply during their own lifetime. Indeed, some have dis-
missed Revelation's judgments as too grotesque and scan-
dalous, and even irreconcilable with the idea of a
merciful God.

Yet God's justice, like His mercy, appears everywhere
in the Bible. It is an integral part of His self-revelation. To
deny the force of divine judgment, then, is to make God
less than God, and to make us less than His children. For
every father must discipline His children, and paternal
discipline is itself a mercy, a fatherly expression of love. In
order to understand the judgment of Revelation—and its

application to our own lives—we need first to understand the covenant bond that unites us to God the Father.

A covenant is a sacred family bond. We can see that God—by His covenants with Adam, Noah, Abraham, Moses, David, and Jesus—gradually extended that family relationship to more and more people. With each covenant came a law; but these were not arbitrary acts of power; they were expressions of fatherly wisdom and love. Every healthy home, after all, has clear guidelines for acceptable and unacceptable behavior. Yet, even more than this, God's law enabled us to love as He Himself loves, to grow in our imitation of the "divine family" of the Blessed Trinity. For Father, Son, and Holy Spirit live eternally in perfect peace and communion.

If God's covenant makes us His family, then sin means more than a broken law. It means broken lives and a broken home. Sin comes from our refusal to keep the covenant, our refusal to love God as much as He loves us. Through sin, we abandon our status as children of God. Sin kills the divine life in us.

Judgment, then, is not an impersonal, legalistic process. It is a matter of love, and it is something we choose for ourselves. Nor is punishment a vindictive act. God's "curses" are not expressions of hatred, but of fatherly love and discipline. Like medicinal ointment, they hurt in order to heal. They impose suffering that is remedial, restorative, and redemptive. God's wrath is an expression of His love for His wayward children.

God is love (1 Jn 4:8), but His love is a consuming fire (Heb 12:29), which stubborn sinners find unbearable. God's fatherhood does not lessen the severity of His wrath or lower the standard of His justice. On the contrary, a loving father requires more from his children than judges demand from defendants. Yet a good father also shows greater mercy.

CAN I HAVE A WITNESS?

We need that understanding of covenant if we're to understand the judgments of the Book of Revelation. And there's no mistaking the situation. John's vision is not merely liturgical, or merely royal, or merely military. It is all these, but it is also juridical. It's a courtroom scene. To citizens of modern democracies, this combination might seem like chaos; but we should remember that, in ancient Israel, the king was commander in chief of the army, chief justice of the courts, and, ideally, high priest as well. As divine king, Jesus fulfilled all these roles par excellence. So, when John sees heaven, he has simultaneously entered the Temple, the throne room, the battlefield, and the courtroom. As in any courtroom, Revelation presents the testimony of sworn witnesses. "And the angel . . . lifted up his right hand to heaven and swore by Him Who lives forever" (Rev 10:5–6). Later, in chapter 11, the court summons Moses and Elijah. Though John does not mention them by name, he suggests their identity by speaking of the powers these men displayed in the Old Testament: in Elijah's case, the power to close up the sky and call down fire; in Moses' case, the ability to turn water to blood and call down plagues. These two witnesses (Rev 11:3) represent the whole of the Law (Moses) and all of the prophets (Elijah). By their presence, they testify that the people of Israel knew full well the obligations of their covenant with God, and the consequences of their infidelity.

Other witnesses testify by giving up their lives. In Greek, the word for "witness" is *martus,* whence we get the word "martyr." Thus, in chapter 6, we encounter "the souls of those who had been slain for the word of God and for the witness they had borne" (v. 9). These witnesses call to the judge for a swift execution of sentence: "O Sovereign Lord, holy and true, how long before You will judge and avenge our blood on those who dwell upon the earth" (6:9–10). Since they cry out from the altar, we know their testimony is true and that it will be heard. But against whom are they testifying? To answer that question, we must consider which city was the source and center of persecution in the Church's first generation—and that was Jerusalem.

PLAGUED BY DOUBT

Jerusalem, it seems, is on trial. God appears as judge (20:11), assisted by angels who sit on twenty thrones (20:4). Throughout the Apocalypse, angels execute the sentence, too, precipitating the destruction of Jerusalem, along with its inhabitants and its Temple. John portrays this event in terms of a terrible Passover. Seven angels pour out the chalices of God's wrath, which issue in seven plagues. The emptying of the chalices (sometimes rendered "cups" or "bowls") is a liturgical action, a libation poured out upon the earth, as wine was poured upon ancient Israel's altar.

In light of the Passover's fulfillment in the Eucharist, this imagery becomes all the more striking. The plagues take place in chapters 15–17 within a liturgical setting: the angels appear with harps, vested as priests in the heavenly Temple, singing the song of Moses and the song of the Lamb (ch. 15). This liturgy means death to God's enemies, yet salvation to His Church. Thus, the angels cry: "For men have shed the blood of saints and prophets, and You have given them blood to drink. It is their due!" (Rev 16:6).

Passover, the Eucharist, and the heavenly liturgy, then, are two-edged swords. While the chalices of the covenant bring life to the faithful, they mean certain death to those who reject the covenant. In the new covenant, as in the old, God gives man the choice between life and death, blessing and curse (see Dt 30:19). To choose the covenant is to choose eternal life in God's family. To reject the new covenant in Christ's blood is to choose one's own death. Jerusalem made that choice, on Passover in A.D. 30. At the time of that Passover, Jesus predicted the end of the world in frightful terms and said, "Truly, this generation shall not pass away till all these things take place" (Mt 24:34). A generation to the ancients (in Greek, *genea*) was forty years. And forty years later, in A.D. 70, a world ended as Jerusalem fell.

FORBIDDEN FRUITS: GRAPES OF WRATH

Why would a merciful God punish in this way? How could we attribute such wrath to the divine Lamb, the very image of mildness? Because God's wrath is a mercy. But to understand this paradox, we first need to explore the psychology of sin, with some help from St. Paul.

Paul's use of the word "wrath" in his Letter to the Romans is illuminating: "For the wrath of God is revealed from heaven against all ungodliness and wickedness of men who by their wickedness suppress the truth. For what can be known about God is plain to them, because God has shown it to them. . . . So they are without excuse; for although they knew God they did not honor Him as God or give thanks to Him, but they became futile in their thinking and their senseless minds were darkened" (Rom 1:18–21).

This could well summarize the "case" against Jerusalem presented in heaven's court: God gave Israel His revelation, indeed the fullness of His revelation in Jesus Christ; yet the people did not honor Him or give thanks to Him; indeed, they suppressed the truth by killing Jesus and persecuting His Church. Thus, "the wrath of God is revealed" ("apocalypsed") against Jerusalem.

What happened then? We read on in Romans: "Therefore God gave them up in the lusts of their hearts to impurity, to the dishonoring of their bodies among themselves" (Rom 1:24). Wait a minute: God gives them up to their vices? He lets them continue sinning?

HOOKED ON A FAILING

Well, yes, and that is a dreadful manifestation of the wrath of God. We might think that the pleasures of sin are preferable to suffering and calamity, but they're not.

We have to recognize sin as the action that destroys our family bond with God and keeps us from life and freedom. How does that happen?

We have an obligation, first, to resist temptation. If we fail then and we sin, we have an obligation to repent immediately. If we do not repent, then God lets us have our way: He allows us to experience the natural consequences of our sins, the illicit pleasures. If we still fail to repent—through self-denial and acts of penance—God allows us to continue in sin, thereby forming a habit, a vice, which darkens our intellect and weakens our will.

Once we're hooked on a sin, our values are turned upside down. Evil becomes our most urgent "good," our deepest longing; good stands as an "evil" because it threatens to keep us from satisfying our illicit desires. At that point, repentance becomes almost impossible, because repentance is, by definition, a turning away from evil and toward the good; but, by now, the sinner has thoroughly redefined both good and evil. Isaiah said of such sinners: "Woe to those who call evil good and good evil" (Is 5:20).

Once we have embraced sin in this way and rejected our covenant with God, only a calamity can save us. Sometimes, the most merciful thing that God can do to a drunk, for example, may be to allow him to wreck his car or be abandoned by his wife—whatever will force him to accept responsibility for his actions.

What happens, though, when an entire nation has fallen into serious and habitual sin? The same principle is at work. God intervenes by allowing economic depression, foreign conquest, or natural catastrophe. Often enough, a nation brings on these disasters by its sins. But, in any case, they are the most merciful of wake-up calls. Sometimes, disaster means that the world the sinners knew must fade away. But, as Jesus said, "What does it profit a man, to gain the whole world and forfeit his life?" (Mk 8:36). It's better to bid farewell to a world of sin than to be lost without hope of repentance.

When people read the Apocalypse, they get frightened by the earthquakes and locusts and famines and scorpions. But the only reason God would allow these things is because He loves us. The world is good—make no mistake about that—but the world is not God. If we've allowed the world and its pleasures to rule us as a god, the best thing the *real* God can do is to start taking away the stones that make up the foundation of our world.

ORDER IN THE COURT

Yet a better world awaits the righteous and the sincerely repentant. To live a good life is not to live free of troubles, but to live free of needless worry. Catastrophes happen to Christians, just as good things seem to happen to wicked people. Yet, for a practicing Christian, even the disasters are good; because they serve to purify us of our attachments to this world. Only when we go bankrupt, perhaps, will we cease to worry about money. Only when we're abandoned by our friends, will we stop trying to impress them. When the money's gone, we can fall back on the one thing that nobody can take away: our God. When our friends don't return our calls, we can, at last, turn to the changeless Friend—Whom we cannot impress, because He knows us thoroughly.

For, as Revelation reveals, the Judge has the goods on us. Judgment isn't just for Jerusalem. "Also another book was opened, which is the book of life. And the dead were judged by what was written in the books, by what they had done" (20:12). One day, you and I will be numbered among "the dead," and we will be judged by what we have done. Elsewhere in Revelation, we see that the saints enter heaven and "their deeds follow them" (14:13). Our works are integral to our salvation; indeed, they'll be the stuff of our judgment.

What's more, we don't have to wait till we're dead to be judged. We stand before the judgment seat whenever we approach heaven, as we do at every Mass. Then, too, do we beg perfect mercy, which is perfect justice, from our heavenly Father. Then, too, do we bind ourselves by covenant with God. Then, too, do we receive the chalice—for our salvation, or for our judgment.

We should recall the judgment of the Apocalypse whenever we hear the words of institution, which are the words of Jesus: "This is the chalice of My blood, the blood of the new and everlasting covenant."

PART THREE

Revelation
for the Masses

ONE

Lifting the Veil

HOW TO SEE THE INVISIBLE

U KRAINIAN CHRISTIANS love to tell the story of
how their ancestors "discovered" the liturgy. In
988, Prince Vladimir of Kiev, upon converting to the Gospel, sent emissaries to Constantinople, the capital city of
Eastern Christendom. There they witnessed the Byzantine liturgy in the cathedral of Holy Wisdom, the
grandest church of the East. After experiencing the
chant, the incense, the icons—but, above all, *the Presence*—the emissaries sent word to the prince: "We did not
know whether we were in heaven or on earth. Never have
we seen such beauty. . . . We cannot describe it, but this
much we can say: there God dwells among mankind."

The Presence. In Greek, the word is *Parousia,* and it
conveys one of the key themes in the Book of Revelation.
In recent centuries, interpreters have used the word al-

most exclusively to denote Jesus' Second Coming at the end of time. That's the only definition you'll find in most English dictionaries. Yet it is not the primary meaning. *Parousia*'s primary meaning is a real, personal, living, lasting, and active presence. In the last line of Matthew's Gospel, Jesus promises, "I will be with you always."

In spite of our redefinitions, the Book of Revelation captures that powerful sense of Jesus' imminent *Parousia*—His coming that takes place *right now*. The Apocalypse shows us that He is here in fullness—in kingship, in judgment, in warfare, in priestly sacrifice, in Body and Blood, Soul and Divinity—whenever Christians celebrate the Eucharist.

"Liturgy is anticipated Parousia, the 'already' entering our 'not yet,'" wrote Cardinal Joseph Ratzinger. When Jesus comes again at the end of time, He will not have a single drop more glory than He has right now upon the altars and in the tabernacles of our churches. God dwells among mankind, *right now*, because the Mass is heaven on earth.

FOR THE RECORD

I want to make clear that this idea—the idea behind this book—is nothing new, and it's certainly not mine. It's as old as the Church, and the Church has never let go of it, though the idea has been lost in the shuffle of doctrinal controversies over the last several centuries.

Nor can we dismiss such talk as the pious wishes of a handful of saints and scholars. For the idea of the Mass as "heaven on earth" is now the explicit teaching of the Catholic faith. You'll find it in several places, for example, in the most fundamental statement of Catholic belief, the *Catechism of the Catholic Church:*

> Christ, indeed, always associates the Church with Himself in this great work [the liturgy] in which God is perfectly glorified and men are sanctified. The Church is His beloved Bride who calls to her Lord and through Him offers worship to the eternal Father . . . [worship] which participates in the liturgy of heaven (no. 1089).

Our liturgy participates in the liturgy of heaven! That's in the *Catechism!* And there's more:

> Liturgy is an "action" of the whole Christ . . . Those who even now celebrate it without signs are already in the heavenly liturgy . . . (no. 1136).

At Mass, we're already in heaven! That's not just me saying so, or a handful of dead theologians. The *Catechism* says so. The *Catechism* also quotes the very passage from Vatican II that affected me so powerfully in the months before my conversion to the Catholic faith:

> In the earthly liturgy we share in a foretaste of that heavenly liturgy which is celebrated in the Holy City of Jerusalem toward which we journey as pilgrims, where Christ is sitting at the right hand of God, Minister of the sanctuary and of the true tabernacle. With all the war-

riors of the heavenly army we sing a hymn of glory to the
Lord . . . (no. 1090).

Warriors, hymns, and holy cities. Now, that's beginning to sound like the Book of Revelation, isn't it? Well,
let the *Catechism* bring it on home:

The Revelation of "what must soon take place," the
Apocalypse, is borne along by the songs of the heavenly
liturgy . . . [T]he Church on earth also sings these
songs with faith in the midst of trial . . . (no. 2642).

All of this the *Catechism* states matter-of-factly, as if it
should be self-evident. Yet, for me, the realization has
been life-changing. To my friends and colleagues, too—
and anyone else I can corner for long enough to deliver a
monologue—this idea, that the Mass is "heaven on
earth," arrives as news, very good news.

LORD JESUS, COME IN GLORY

If we want to see the liturgy as Prince Vladimir's emissaries saw it, we must learn to see the Apocalypse as the
Church sees it. If we want to make sense of the Apocalypse, we have to learn to read it with a sacramental imagination. When we look into these matters once again,
now with new eyes of faith, we will see the sense amid the
strangeness in the Book of Revelation, we will see the
glory hidden in the mundane in next Sunday's Mass.

Look again and discover that the golden thread of

liturgy is what holds together the apocalyptic pearls of
John's vision:

Sunday worship	1:10
a high priest	1:13
an altar	8:3–4; 11:1; 14:18
priests *(presbyteroi)*	4:4; 11:15; 14:3; 19:4
vestments	1:13; 4:4; 6:11; 7:9; 15:6; 19:13–14
consecrated celibacy	14:4
lamp stands, or Menorah	1:12; 2:5
penitence	ch. 2 and 3
incense	5:8; 8:3–5
the book, or scroll	5:1
the Eucharistic Host	2:17
chalices	15:7; ch. 16; 21:9
the Sign of the Cross (the *tau*)	7:3; 14:1; 22:4
the Gloria	15:3–4
the Alleluia	19:1, 3, 4, 6
Lift up your hearts	11:12
the "Holy, Holy, Holy"	4:8
the Amen	19:4; 22:21
the "Lamb of God"	5:6 and throughout
the prominence of the Virgin Mary	12:1–6; 13–17
intercession of angels and saints	5:8; 6:9–10; 8:3–4

devotion to St. Michael, archangel	12:7
antiphonal chant	4:8–11; 5:9–14; 7:10–12; 18:1–8
readings from Scripture	ch. 2–3; 5; 8:2–11
the priesthood of the faithful	1:6; 20:6
catholicity, or universality	7:9
silent contemplation	8:1
the marriage supper of the Lamb	19:9, 17

Taken together, these elements comprise much of the Apocalypse—and most of the Mass. Other liturgical elements in Revelation are easier for modern readers to miss. For example, few people today know that trumpets and harps were the standard instruments for liturgical music in John's day, as organs are today in the West. And throughout John's vision, the angels and Jesus pronounce blessings using standard liturgical formulas: "Blessed is he who . . ." If you go back and read Revelation end to end, you'll also notice that all of God's great historical interventions—plagues, wars, and so on—follow closely upon liturgical actions: hymns, doxologies, libations, incensing.

Yet, the Mass is not *just* in selected small details. It's in the grand scheme, too. We can see, for instance, that the Apocalypse, like the Mass, divides rather neatly in half. The first eleven chapters concern themselves with the proclamation of the letters to the seven churches and the opening of the scroll. This emphasis on "readings" makes Part One a close match for the Liturgy of the Word. Significantly, the first three chapters of Revelation mark a sort of Penitential Rite; in the seven letters to the churches, Jesus uses the word "repent" eight times. For me, this recalls the words of the ancient *Didache*, the liturgical manual of the first century: "first confess your transgressions, that your sacrifice may be pure." Even John's opening assumes that the book will be read aloud by a lector within the liturgical assembly: "Blessed is he who reads aloud the words of this prophecy, and blessed are those who hear" (Rev 1:3).

Revelation's second half begins in chapter 11 with the opening of God's temple in heaven, and culminates in the pouring of the seven chalices and the marriage supper of the Lamb. With the opening of heaven, the chalices, and the banquet, Part Two offers a striking image of the Liturgy of the Eucharist.

EXTRASENSORY CENSERS?

In the Apocalypse, John depicts celestial scenes in graphic, earthly terms, and we have every right to ask *why*. Why depict spiritual worship—which certainly doesn't involve harps or censers—with such vivid sensory impressions? Why not use mathematical figures, as other ancient mystics did, so that readers would understand the truly esoteric, transcendent, and immaterial nature of heavenly worship?

I suspect that God revealed heavenly worship in earthly terms so that humans—who, for the first time, were invited to participate in heavenly worship—would know how to do it. I'm not saying that the Church sat around waiting for the Apocalypse to drop from heaven, so that Christians would know how to worship. No, the Apostles and their successors had been celebrating the liturgy since Pentecost, at least. Yet neither is Revelation merely an echo of a liturgy already established, a projection into heaven of what's happening on earth.

Revelation is an *unveiling;* that's the literal meaning of the Greek word *apokalypsis*. The book is a visionary reflection that reveals a norm. With the destruction of Jerusalem, the Church was definitively leaving behind a beautiful temple, a holy city, and a venerable priesthood. Yes, Christians were embracing a New Covenant, which somehow *concluded* the old, but somehow also *included* the old. What should they bring with them, from the old worship to the new? What should they leave behind? Revelation gave them guidance.

Some things had been clearly replaced in the new dispensation. Israel marked its covenant by circumcising male children on the eighth day; the Church sealed the New Covenant by baptism. Israel celebrated the sabbath as a day of rest and worship; the Church celebrated the Lord's day, Sunday, the day of resurrection. Israel recalled the old Passover once a year; the Church reenacted the definitive Passover of Jesus Christ in its celebration of the Eucharist.

Yet Jesus did not intend to do away with all that was

in the Old Covenant; that's why He established a Church. He came to intensify, internationalize, and internalize the worship of Israel. Thus, the incarnation invested many of the trappings of the Old Covenant with greater capacities. For example, there would no longer be a central sanctuary on earth. Revelation shows that Christ the King is enthroned in heaven, where He acts as high priest in the Holy of Holies. But does that mean the Church can't have buildings, or officers, or candlesticks, or chalices, or vestments? No. Revelation's clear answer is that we can have all of these—all these, and heaven, too.

ZION AURA

But everyone knew where to find Jerusalem. Where would they find heaven? Apparently, not very far away from old Jerusalem. The Letter to the Hebrews says: "But you have come to *Mount Zion* and to the city of the living God, *the heavenly Jerusalem,* and to innumerable angels in festal gathering, and to the assembly of the firstborn who are enrolled in heaven, and to a judge Who is God of all, and to the spirits of just men made perfect, and to Jesus, the mediator of a new covenant, and to the sprinkled blood that speaks more graciously than the blood of Abel" (Heb 12:21–24).

That little paragraph neatly summarizes the entire Apocalypse: the communion of saints and angels, the feast, the judgment, and the blood of Christ. But where does it *leave* us? Just where the Apocalypse did: "Then I looked, and lo, *on Mount Zion* stood the Lamb, and with

Him a hundred and forty-four thousand who had His name and His Father's name written on their foreheads" (Rev 14:1).

All our Scriptural roads seem to lead to the city of King David, Mount Zion. God blessed Zion abundantly in the Old Covenant. "For the Lord has chosen Zion; He has desired it for His habitation: 'This is my resting place forever; here I will dwell'" (Ps 132:13–14). "I have set my king on Zion, my holy hill" (Ps 2:6). In Zion, God would establish the royal house of David, whose kingdom would last for all ages. There, God Himself would dwell forever among His people.

Remember that Zion was also the place where Jesus instituted the Eucharist, and where the Holy Spirit descended on Pentecost. Thus, the "holy hill" was even more favored in the second dispensation. The Last Supper and Pentecost were the two events that sealed the New Covenant.

Notice, too, that the remnant of Israel, the 144,000 in Revelation 14, appear on Mount Zion—though in Revelation 7 they're shown in the heavenly Jerusalem. That's an odd discrepancy. Where were they, really: on Zion or in heaven? Look again to Hebrews 12 for the answer: "you have come to *Mount Zion . . . the heavenly Jerusalem.*" Mount Zion *is* the heavenly Jerusalem, because the events that took place are what brought about the definitive union of heaven and earth.

The church on the site of these events survived the destruction of Jerusalem, but only as a sign. For the Christians of Judea, the site of the upper room was the "little church of God" dedicated to King David and St.

James, the first bishop of Jerusalem. It was a "house church," where believers met to break bread and to pray. Beyond that, however, Zion had become the living symbol of the New Covenant, and that's how it was enshrined forever in the Book of Revelation. Zion is a symbol of our earthly point of contact with heaven.

Today, even though we are thousands of miles from that little hill in Israel, we are there with Jesus in the upper room, and we are there with Jesus in heaven, whenever we go to Mass.

FIRST COMES LOVE, THEN COMES MARRIAGE

This is what was unveiled in the Book of Revelation: the union of heaven and earth, consummated in the Holy Eucharist. The first word of the book suggests as much. The term *apokalypsis,* usually translated as "revelation," literally means "unveiling." In John's time, Jews commonly used *apokalypsis* to describe part of their week-long wedding festivities. The *apokalypsis* was the lifting of the veil of a virgin bride, which took place immediately before the marriage was consummated in sexual union.

And that's what John was getting at. So close is the unity of heaven and earth that it is like the fruitful and ecstatic union of a husband and wife in love. St. Paul describes the Church as the bride of Christ (see Eph 5)— and Revelation unveils that bride. The climax of the Apocalypse, then, is the communion of the Church and Christ: the marriage supper of the Lamb (Rev 19:9). From that moment, man rises up from the earth to worship in heaven. "Then I fell down at [the angel's] feet to worship him," John writes, "but he said to me, 'You must not do that! I am a fellow servant with you and your brethren who hold the testimony of Jesus' " (Rev 19:10). Remember that Israel's tradition always had men worshiping *in imitation of angels.* Now, as Revelation shows, both heaven and earth participate together in a single act of loving worship.

This apocalypse, or unveiling, points back to the cross. Matthew reports that, when Jesus died, "the curtain [or veil] of the Temple was torn in two, from top to bottom" (27:51). Thus, the sanctuary of God was "apocalypsed," unveiled, His dwelling no longer reserved for the high priest alone. Jesus' redemption unveiled the Holy of Holies, opening God's presence to everyone. Heaven and earth could now embrace in intimate love.

THE OLD SCHOOL

The ancient liturgies were saturated with the language of heaven on earth. The Liturgy of St. James declares: "we have been counted worthy to enter into the place of the tabernacle of Your glory, and to be within the veil, and to behold the Holy of Holies." The Liturgy of Saints Addai and Mari adds: "How awesome today is this place! For this is none other than the house of God and the gate of heaven; because You have been seen eye to eye, O Lord."

St. Cyril of Jerusalem (fifth century) offers a profound meditation on the line "Lift up your hearts!" "For truly," he says, "in that most awesome hour, we should have our hearts on high with God, and not below, thinking of earth and earthly things. The Priest bids all in that hour to dismiss all cares of this life, or household worries, and to have their hearts in heaven with the merciful God."

Indeed, we must be like St. John on Patmos, when he heard the voice from heaven say, "Come up here" (see Rev 11:12). That's what it means to "Lift up your hearts!" It means to open our hearts to the heaven that's before us, just as St. John did. Lift up your hearts, then, to worship in the Spirit. For, in the liturgy, says the fourth-century *Liber Graduum,* "the body is a hidden temple, and the heart is a hidden altar for the ministry in Spirit."

First, however, we must actively seek recollection. St. Cyril goes on: "But let no one come here who could say with his mouth, 'We lift up our hearts unto the Lord,' but have his mind concerned with the cares of this life. At all times, God should be in our memory. But if this is impossible by reason of human frailty, we should at least make the effort in that hour."

Put simply, we should heed the compact phrase of the Byzantine liturgy: "Wisdom! Be attentive!"

KNOCK, KNOCK

Yes, be attentive! Because Revelation is unveiling more than "information." It's a personal invitation, intended for you and me from all eternity. The Revelation of Jesus Christ has an *immediate* and *overwhelming* impact on our lives. *We* are the bride of Christ unveiled; *we* are His Church. And Jesus wants each and every one of us to enter into the most intimate relationship imaginable with Him. He uses wedding imagery to demonstrate how much He loves us, how close He wants us to stay—and how permanent he intends our union to be.

Behold, God makes all things new. The Book of Revelation is not as strange as it seems, and the Mass is richer than we'd ever dreamed. Revelation is as familiar as the life we live; and even the dullest Mass is suddenly paved with gold and glittering jewels.

You and I need to open our eyes and rediscover this long-lost secret of the Church, the early Christians' key to understanding the mysteries of the Mass, the only true key to the mysteries of the Apocalypse. "It is in this eternal liturgy that the Spirit and the Church enable us to participate whenever we celebrate the mystery of salvation in the sacraments" *(Catechism,* no. 1139).

We go to heaven—not only when we die, or when we go to Rome, or when we make a pilgrimage to the Holy Land. *We go to heaven when we go to Mass.* This is not merely a symbol, not a metaphor, not a parable, not a figure of speech. It is real. In the fourth century, St. Athanasius wrote, "My beloved brethren, it is no temporal feast that we come to, but an eternal, heavenly feast. We do not display it in shadows; we approach it in reality."

Heaven on earth—that's reality! That's where you stood and where you dined last Sunday! What were you thinking then?

Consider what the Lord wanted you to think. Consider His invitations from the Book of Revelation: "He who has an ear, let him hear what the Spirit says to the churches. To him who conquers I will give some of the *hidden manna*" (2:17). What is the hidden manna? Remember the promise Jesus made when He spoke of "manna" in John's Gospel: "Your fathers ate the manna in the wilderness, and they died. This is the bread which comes down from heaven, that a man may eat of it and not die. I am the living bread which came down from heaven" (6:49–51). Manna was the daily bread of God's people during their pilgrimage in the desert. Now, Jesus is offering something greater, and He's quite specific about His invitation: "Behold, I stand at the door and knock; if anyone hears My voice and opens the door, I will come in to him *and eat with him,* and he with Me" (3:20).

So Jesus really does have a meal on His mind; He wants to share the hidden manna with us, and He *is* the hidden manna. In Revelation 4:1, we see, too, that this is more than an intimate dinner for two. Jesus had stood at the door and knocked, and now the door is open. John enters "the Spirit" to see priests, martyrs, and angels gathered around heaven's throne. With John, we discover that heaven's banquet is a family meal.

Now, with eyes of faith—and "in the Spirit"—let us begin to see that Revelation invites us to a heavenly banquet, to a love embrace, to Zion, to judgment, to battle. To Mass.

TWO

Worship Is Warfare

WHICH WILL YOU CHOOSE: FIGHT OR FLIGHT?

H UMAN KIND," said the poet T. S. Eliot, "cannot bear very much reality." We need not look far for proof of this assertion. Real life, today, is what people flee, one by one, each retreating into his private distraction. The escape routes range from drugs and alcohol to romance novels and virtual-reality games.

What is it about reality that humankind finds so unbearable? It is the enormity of evil, its seeming omnipresence and power, and our own apparent inability to escape it—indeed, our inability to avoid *perpetrating* evil. Hell, it seems, is everywhere—in sham imitation of God's omnipresence—threatening to consume us, to suffocate us.

This is the reality we cannot bear. Yet this is the stark and terrible reality that John portrayed, without flinching, in Revelation. John's beasts loom monstrous, beyond

Hollywood's darkest imaginings, snapping their jaws at the most innocent and vulnerable prey: a pregnant woman, a baby boy. They despise both nature and grace, Church and state. They can sweep a third of the stars from the sky. They're the power behind the throne in nations and empires. They grow strong from the immorality of the people they seduce; they get drunk on the "wine" of their victims' fornication, greed, and abusive power.

FIGHT OR FLIGHT?

Facing such opposition, we must choose: either fight or flight. This is a basic human instinct. Moreover, after a superficial evaluation of our own apparent resources, and the enemy's apparent resources, "flight" might seem the reasonable choice. According to the spiritual masters, however, flight is not a real option. In his classic work, *The Spiritual Combat,* Dom Lorenzo Scupoli wrote: "This war is unavoidable, and you must either fight or die. The obstinacy of your enemies is so fierce that peace and arbitration with them is utterly impossible." In short: we can run from evil, but we can't hide.

Moreover, we cannot ascend to heaven if we flee the battle. God has destined us, the Church, to be the Bride of the Lamb. Yet we cannot rule if we do not first conquer the forces that oppose us, the powers who are pretenders to our throne.

What are we to do? We should take a look around us, after lifting the veil of mere human sight. John reveals the most encouraging news for Christians in battle. Two thirds of the angels are on our side, fighting constantly, even while we sleep. St. Michael the Archangel, heaven's fiercest warrior, is our untiring and unbeatable ally. All the saints in heaven constantly call to almighty God for our vindication. And—most encouraging of all—in the end we win! John sees the battle from the perspective of eternity, so he can reveal the ending as vividly as he describes the casualties. The battles rage so fiercely that rivers run red with blood and corpses lie rotting in heaps in the streets. Yet the victors enter a city whose streams flow with living water and whose sun never sets.

Hear Father Scupoli again: "if the fury of your enemies is great, and their numbers overwhelming, the love which God holds for you is infinitely greater. The angel who protects you and the saints who intercede for you are more numerous."

SOCIETY PAGES

We can count on heavenly help. Who can ask for greater assurance? Yet we often do. Many Christians remain troubled because they perceive that Jesus has somehow "delayed" in coming to help them. This seems especially true when they look at society's degeneracy. The world, sometimes, seems firmly in the hands of evil forces, and despite the prayers of Christians, the evil remains and even prospers.

Still, Revelation shows that it is the saints and angels who direct history by their prayers. More than Washington, D.C., more than the United Nations, more than Wall Street, more than any place you can name, power belongs to the saints of the Most High gathered around the throne of the Lamb. The blood of the martyrs calls to God for vengeance (Rev 6:9–10), and He vindicates them, now as at the dawn of history, when Abel's blood cried out from the earth. It is the saints' prayers that immediately call forth the wrath of the Lamb against "the great men . . . the rich and the strong" (6:15–16).

Yet the power of the saints is of a different order than the world's idea of power, and the wrath of the Lamb differs significantly from human vengeance. That may seem self-evident, but it's worth our deepest contemplation. For many Christians profess to believe in a heavenly sort of power, which, on closer analysis, turns out to be worldly power writ large.

Consider, for a moment, Jesus' Jewish contemporaries and their worldly expectation of the Messiah: He would establish the kingdom of God by military and political means—conquer Rome, subjugate the gentiles, and so on. We know that such hopes were dashed away. Rather than marching on Jerusalem with His armies, Jesus waged a campaign of mercy and love, manifested by the meals shared with tax collectors and other sinners.

And we all learned our lesson, right? It doesn't seem that way. Because, today, many Christians still hope for the same messianic vengeance as the first-century Jews. Though Christ came peacefully the first time, they say, He'll come back with a holy vengeance in the end, crushing His foes with almighty force.

YOU CALL THIS WRATH?

But what if Jesus' Second Coming turned out to be much like His first? Would many Christians be disappointed? Perhaps, but I don't think we should be. For, even though Revelation narrates a fair share of famines and plagues and pestilences, still chapter 6 portrays God's judgment of the mighty and powerful as the "wrath of the Lamb." Why does John use the lamb image here? What kind of terror can a lamb really inspire? Why didn't he speak of the wrath of the Lion of Judah?

Similarly, why is "overcoming" accomplished after Christ's first coming by those who "loved not their lives even unto death"? Or why are the opposing sides set forth so unevenly: two dragons and a land-beast attack the pregnant woman as she gives birth to the baby Messiah? Sure, there's St. Michael the Archangel; but the best he can do is kick the dragon out of heaven—so now the devil's free to pursue the woman into the wilderness and then make war on the rest of her offspring. In short, the deck is clearly stacked—the wrong way!

Then, what about the closing scene (ch. 19), when Christ comes to "avenge the blood of His servants" (v. 2)? There, we see someone named "Faithful and True" riding on a white horse, accompanied by heavenly hosts in white linen (is this their best armor?), fighting with nothing but a sword—"coming out of his mouth"! Why is it not in His right hand? Why isn't He swinging it? Clearly, it's the sword of the Spirit, the Word of God, which He's preaching—and not a military weapon of mass destruction. Then, He takes the Beast and False Prophet, and throws them alive into the fire and brimstone. Note that He doesn't kill them first, doesn't cut them up or gloat over their corpses. Next, the fate of the wicked is described in the following two chapters simply in terms of their being excluded from the New Jerusalem. What kind of comeuppance is this? Why is Jesus still a Lamb—till the very end? And why a marriage supper, rather than a victory party?

I would suggest that the expectations of many Christians about Christ's Second Coming may stand in need of adjustment. Otherwise, we can find ourselves fighting disappointment—as did Jesus' Jewish contemporaries in the first century. Perhaps we need to rethink the common image of God suppressing his wrath—"Just you wait, you'll see how angry and vengeful I can really be"—by viewing it more carefully in light of His perfect fatherhood. This does not do away with divine wrath; it simply fits it into the consistent picture of God that Jesus provides. As I said earlier, viewing God's judgment in terms of divine fatherhood does not lower the standard of justice, or lessen the severity of judgment; fathers generally require more from their sons and daughters than judges from defendants.

What, then, should be our image of Jesus' Second Coming? For me, it is Eucharistic, and it is brought about as the Mass brings heaven to earth. Just as the earthly priest stands over the bread and wine and says "This is My body," thus transforming the elements, so Christ the high priest stands over the cosmos, pronouncing the same words. We stand on the earth as the elements stand on the altar. We are here to be transformed: to die to self, live for others, and love like God. That is what's happening on the altar of the earth, just as it happens on the altars of our churches. As the fire descended from heaven to consume the sacrifices on Solomon's altar, so the fire descended to consume the disciples at the first Pentecost. The fire is one and the same; it is the Holy Spirit, Who enables us to be offered up as living sacrifices upon the altar of the earth. That is what makes sense out of the second half of the Apocalypse.

HISTORY'S BRIDAL PATH

It makes sense, too, out of the events of our everyday lives. In the light of divine fire, we see the daily news not as meaningless and unconnected sound bites, but as a story, whose ending we already know. All things in history—in world history and in our personal history—work together for the good of those who love God (see Rom 8:28). For Christ is Lord of history, its beginning (see Jn 1:1) and its end (see 1 Cor 4:5).

Christ is firmly in charge, and He wants us to reign with Him as His bride. Thus, we must fight to gain our throne, but our warfare is hardly grim. We can even look upon it in romantic terms. History is the story of Christ wooing His Church, gradually drawing us all to our marriage supper, the banquet of the Lamb. He looks upon us as Adam looked upon Eve and says, "This at last is bone of my bones and flesh of my flesh" (Gen 2:23). The Church is at once His bride and His body, for in marriage

the two become *one* flesh (see Mt 19:5). Thus, Christ
looks at us and says, "This is *My* body."

God intends all of history—whether the particular
events seem good or ill for "our side"—to lead us to the
eternal communion of our marriage supper. We must not
underestimate Christ's desire for us to arrive at the feast.
Remember He is a bridegroom awaiting His bride. So the
passionate words He spoke to His Apostles are true for us
as well: "I have earnestly desired to eat this Passover with
you" (Lk 22:15).

Nor must we underestimate Jesus' power to lead us
to the feast. He, after all, is God almighty, all-knowing.
Eternal communion with the Church is what He wants,
and what He wills, and it is surely what He accomplishes
even now. Loving communion with His Church is the
very reason that God became a man and bled and died;
and it is the very reason He created the world in the first
place. Thus, all the events of all time should lead us, inex-
orably, to the event we see mystically in the last chapters
of the Book of Revelation.

RESISTING A REST

Hell, then, may seem to prevail in the world, but it does
not. The Church is, in a sense, in charge. Our prayers,
and especially the sacrifice of the Mass, are the force that
propels history toward its goal. In fact, in the sacrifice of
the Mass, history achieves its goal, because there Christ
and the Church celebrate their wedding feast and con-
summate their marriage.

How, then, should we understand our ongoing combat? If history has, in a sense, already reached its goal, why should we continue to fight? Because not all the world has come to the feast, even if you and I have. So we must continue to ransom the time, to restore all things in Christ. Remember that when we go to Mass, we take along all our professional work, family life, sufferings, and leisure, and all of these become spiritual sacrifices acceptable to God through Jesus Christ, during the celebration of the Eucharist. God wills that you and I should play an indispensable role in salvation history. "The Spirit and the Bride say, 'Come' " (Rev 22:17). Note that it's not just the Spirit Who issues the call to mankind, but *the Spirit and the Bride*. The Bride is the Church—it's you and me.

Meanwhile, our enemy, the Beast, consecrates nothing. He works tirelessly, sometimes intimidating us by his industry; but his labors are sterile. He is 666, the creature stalled in the sixth day, perpetually in travail, yet never reaching the seventh day of sabbath rest and worship.

So the battle goes on, and we have enlisted for active duty. We must, however, begin the fighting very close to home. Our most dangerous enemies are those we'll find in our own soul: pride, envy, laziness, gluttony, greed, anger, and lust. Before we can advance on enemies in society at large, we need to identify our own sinful habits and begin to root them out. All the while, we need to grow in the wisdom and virtue that make us more like Christ.

We can advance only if we come to know ourselves as we really are, that is, as we appear to almighty God. When

John faced the Lamb of God, he accurately sized up the situation, and he fell down to the ground in humility. We need to see the truth with the same clarity. Thus we need to see matters in the same divine light. Yet how can we, when all around we're beset by darkness? The only way is for us to step into that same clean, well-lighted place where John had his vision: worship in the Spirit on the Lord's day—which is, at the same time, the heavenly city where "night shall be no more" (Rev 22:5).

Only in the new Jerusalem will we see ourselves as we are, for there we will face judgment; there we will read what is written in the book of life. It's heaven, but we don't need to die to go there. The new Jerusalem is Mount Zion; it is the Church of the Upper Room; and it touches down for us in the Holy Mass.

CAN'T STAND UP FOR FALLING DOWN

We want to know ourselves. So we must *use well* the parts of the Mass that are set apart for self-examination: the penitential rite, for example, with the "Lord, Have Mercy" and "I Confess." This requires *recollection,* an interior quiet that allows us to examine our thoughts, words, and deeds. If we want to be recollected, it helps to arrive at church well before Mass and begin our prayer. Interior recollection will enable us to concentrate on the reality of the Mass, no matter what's going on around us: come crying babies, bad music, or mediocre homilies.

To prepare for Mass, we should also take frequent advantage of the Sacrament of Reconciliation, confessing our sins after making a deep examination of conscience.

Remember the counsel of the *Didache,* the Church's oldest liturgical guide: we should make confession before
receiving the Eucharist, so that our sacrifice may be pure.
Though the Church only *requires* us to confess once a
year, the overwhelming teaching of the saints and popes
is that we should go "frequently." How often is that?
That will vary according to your circumstances and the
advice of your priest-confessor. We should follow good
example, however, knowing that most saints went at least
weekly, and the most trusted spiritual masters advise a
monthly minimum.

If we are honest before God, then, we'll find ourselves, in our hearts, falling down in humility, as John did.
We will pray with perfect sincerity the prayer before Communion: "Lord, I am not worthy to receive you. . . ."

IT'S CROWDED IN HERE

What do we see when we stand in light? We see that we
are sinners and we are weak; but we see much more as
well.

We see that, in this war, we are the stronger side by
far. At Mass, we invoke the angels, and we worship beside
them, as John did—as their equals before God! We call
upon their help. Listen closely to the preface of the Mass,
just before you sing the "Holy, Holy, Holy": "Now, with
angels and archangels, and the whole company of
heaven, we sing the unending hymn of Your praise."
Some Eastern liturgies even dare to number the angels:
"a thousand thousands and ten thousand times ten thousand hosts of angels and archangels." The word "hosts"

in this context connotes military might—like "legions" or "divisions." The Mass, it seems, is like the Normandy invasion in the spiritual realm.

We also invoke the saints, acknowledging them by name. In the Roman Canon, *Eucharistic Prayer I,* the priest reads off a long list of Apostles, popes, martyrs, and other saints—twenty-four, to correspond exactly to the *presbyteroi* surrounding God's throne in the Apocalypse.

In spiritual warfare, the saints are powerful allies. Remember that, in Revelation, God's vengeance follows close upon the prayers of the martyrs beneath His altar. In some Eastern liturgies—for example, the ancient Liturgy of St. Mark—the congregations echo the martyrs' prayers: "Crush under our feet Satan, and all his wicked influence. Humble now, as at all times, the enemies of Your Church. Lay bare their pride. Speedily show them their weakness. Bring to naught the wicked plots they contrive against us. Arise, O Lord, and let Your enemies be scattered, and let all who hate Your holy name be put to flight."

No doubt, we've got power and might on our side. We say so in the "Holy, Holy, Holy," which we sing, together with the angels, at every Mass we attend. We should make sure to give that song all we've got. Did you ever watch a strong army march in formation? The soldiers move with unified precision, and they chant with gusto and confidence. That's how we should proceed through the liturgy: confidently, joyfully. It's not that we deny the enemy's strength; we just glory in the fact that God is stronger, and God is our strength!

SEND THE DEMONS SCREAMIN'

Knowing ourselves and the angels, of course, is not enough. We must come to know God more and more, and that is an endless (and endlessly rewarding) pursuit. Because the more we learn about Him, the more we realize we don't know, and can't know without grace.

Coming to know God, we will come to know what infinite strength and resources we can call upon in battle. So we should prepare for Mass, throughout our lives, by ongoing doctrinal and spiritual formation. No soldier would rush untrained into battle. Neither should we think that we can conquer demons if we're flabby in our faith. We need to put ourselves through the rigors of basic training, living a sustained and disciplined life of prayer, and studying the faith daily, reading the Bible, using Catholic tapes, TV, and books (especially the *Catechism of the Catholic Church*). All this is a lifelong task.

Our doctrinal study will invest the liturgy's every word and gesture with power. We will make the Sign of the Cross, *knowing* that it is the banner we carry into battle—and before that banner, demons tremble. We will dip our fingers into the holy water, *knowing*, in the words of St. Teresa of Ávila, that this water makes demons flee. We will recite every line of the Gloria and the Creed as if our lives depended on it, because they do.

And what "happens" on the battlefield when we receive Jesus Christ, King of Kings and Lord of Lords, in Holy Communion? The saints tell us that we rout the enemy at that moment, and that ever afterward we can keep watch *with Jesus' watchfulness.* A fifth-century monk of Mount Sinai testified that "when that fire enters us, it at once drives the evil spirits from our heart and remits the sins we have previously committed. . . . And if after this, standing at the entrance to our heart, we keep strict watch over the intellect, when we are again permitted to receive those Mysteries, the divine body will illumine our intellect still more and make it shine like a star."

So the brightness of the Mass goes home with us as the perpetual day of the heavenly Jerusalem. As we grow in grace, our Mass becomes a light burning within us, too, even amid our work and family life. That's security in wartime; for the weaker army will rarely attack in the light of day. And the devil knows, when the light of Christ is on one side of the battle, the darkness of hell is the weaker.

D-DAY

Yet the battle remains a battle. Even if our victory is assured, the fighting itself won't necessarily be easy, and this is especially true at Mass. Knowing the power of grace, the devil will most forcefully assault us, says one ancient teacher, "at the time of the great feasts and during the Divine Liturgy—especially when we are intending to receive Holy Communion."

What is our particular combat during Mass? Maybe it's warding off contempt for the worshiper whose perfume is too strong, or the man who sings the wrong lyrics off-key. Maybe it's holding back our judgment against the parishioner who's skipping out early. Maybe it's turning the other way when we begin to wonder how low that neckline really goes. Maybe it's fighting off smugness when we hear a homily riddled with grammatical errors. Maybe it's smiling, in an understanding way, at the mom with the screaming baby.

Those are the tough battles. Maybe they're not as romantic as sabers clashing in a faraway desert, or marching through tear gas to protest injustice. But because they're so perfectly hidden, so *interior,* they require greater heroism. No one but God and His angels will notice that you didn't mentally critique Father's homily this week. No one but God and His angels will notice that you withheld judgment against the family that was underdressed. So you don't get a medal; you win a battle instead.

REALITY CHECK—BEAR IT

The reality "unveiled" in John's Apocalypse is as terrifying as it is consoling. Yet the good news is that, with heavenly help, we can bear it. We are children of the King of the universe; but we live amid constant peril, surrounded by dark spiritual forces who want to destroy our souls, our crown, and our birthright.

Yet the winning is ours for the taking. How right that our tradition associates the Mass with the *todah,* ancient Israel's thanksgiving sacrifice. The *todah* was an expression of complete confidence: a prayer for deliverance from one's enemies, a prayer for deliverance from imminent death—and, at the same time, the *todah* offered thanks that God would answer one's prayers. Recall, too, how the rabbis predicted that, in the messianic age, all sacrifice would cease except the *todah*. Thus we pray with confidence in every Mass, "deliver us from evil"; and thus we give glory to God for our deliverance.

In Holy Communion, we receive the Bread that will sustain us, even during the enemy's longest siege. In the Mass, as we stand beside our heavenly allies, the devil is impotent. Before the altar, we approach heaven, the fount of infinite grace, which alone can change our sinful hearts. At the marriage supper of the Lamb, we ourselves are enthroned to reign over history by our prayers.

In this millennial season, many people will come to you shouting that the end is near, and that the latest skirmish across the sea is surely the battle of Armageddon. Don't be frightened. You can tell them that, yes, the end is near; yes, the Apocalypse is now. But the Church has *always* taught that the end is near—as near as your parish church. And it's something you should be running *to*, not *from*.

Any battle we're impatient to fight with earthly weapons we should first enter with weapons of the spirit. You want justice for oppressed people across the globe? You want relief for the martyrs overseas? Don't rush first to city hall. If you want to bring about the kingdom, you should first worship well, as often as you can, wherever the sanctuary of the King touches down in the Mass.

THREE

Parish the Thought

REVELATION
AS FAMILY PORTRAIT

H EAVEN IS A FAMILY REUNION with all God's children; and this is true, too, of heaven on earth: the Holy Mass. Let's go back to that telling passage from Hebrews: "You have come to Mount Zion . . . the heavenly Jerusalem . . . and to the assembly of *the firstborn* who are enrolled in heaven" (Heb 12:22–23). Heaven touches earth in the Mass and encompasses the family of God Himself.

In Revelation, John only intensifies the image. John describes our communion with Christ in the most remarkably intimate terms, as "the marriage supper of the Lamb" (Rev 19:9).

FAMILY HISTORY

Yet, before we can understand this family bond, many of us will have to put aside our modern, Western notions about family. We live in a time when families are highly mobile; few people will die in the town where they were born. We live in a time when families are small; fewer children today experience uncles and aunts and countless cousins, as previous generations did. When moderns say "family," we usually mean the nuclear family: mom, dad, and a child or two.

To appreciate John's vision, though, we have to glimpse a much different world, a world in which the large, extended family defined the world of a given individual. The family—the tribe, the clan—was a man or woman's primary identity, dictating where they would live, how they would work, and whom they might marry. Often, people wore a conspicuous sign of their family identity, such as a signet ring or a distinguishing mark on the body.

A nation in the ancient world was largely a network of such families, as Israel comprised the twelve tribes named for Jacob's sons. Unifying each family was the bond of *covenant*, the wider culture's idea of what constituted human relations, rights, duties, and loyalties. When a family welcomed new members, through marriage or some other alliance, both parties—the new members and the established tribe—would seal the covenant bond by swearing a solemn oath, sharing a common meal, or offering a sacrifice.

God's relationship with Israel was defined by a covenant, and Jesus described His relationship with the Church in the same terms. At the Last Supper, He blessed the cup of the *New Covenant* in His blood (see Mt 26:28; Mk 14:24; Lk 22:20; 1 Cor 11:25).

The Book of Revelation makes clear that this New Covenant is the closest and most intimate of family bonds. John's vision concludes with the marriage supper of the Lamb and His bride, the Church. With this event, we Christians seal and renew our family relationship with God Himself. In our bodies, we bear the mark of God's tribe. We call God Himself our true Brother, our Father, our Spouse.

THE GOD WHO IS FAMILY

In the Book of Revelation, believers bear the mark of this supernatural family upon their brow. The early Christians, for centuries, reminded themselves of this reality by tracing the Sign of the Cross on their foreheads. We do the same thing when we make the Sign of the Cross today; we mark our bodies "in the name of" our divine family: the Father, Son, and Holy Spirit. Thus, in the Apocalypse as in the Mass, the family of God—like any traditional family in ancient Israel—finds its identity in the family's name and in its sign.

Yet here's the most remarkable revelation: our family is not only *named for* God—our family *is* God. Christianity is the only religion whose one God is a family. His most proper name is Father, Son, and Holy Spirit. Said Pope John Paul II: "God in His deepest mystery is not a solitude, but a family, since He has in Himself fatherhood, sonship, and the essence of the family, which is love."

To me, that's an earth-shaking truth. Notice he did not say that God is *like* a family, but that He *is* a family. Why? Because God possesses, from eternity, the essential attributes of family—fatherhood, sonship, and love—and He alone possesses them in their perfection. It may be more accurate, then, to say that the Hahns (or any household) are like a family, since our family has these attributes, but only imperfectly.

God is a family, and we are His. By establishing the New Covenant, Christ founded one Church—His mystical body—as an extension of His Incarnation. By taking on flesh, Christ divinized flesh, and He extended the Trinity's life to all humanity, through the Church. Incorporated into the Body of Christ, we become "sons in the Son." We become children in the eternal household of God. We share in the life of the Trinity.

The Catholic Church is nothing less than the universal Family of God.

AN AFFINITY FOR THE TRINITY

As Catholics, we renew our covenant-family bond in the marriage supper of the Lamb—an action that is, at once, a shared meal, a sacrifice, and an oath (a sacrament). The Apocalypse unveiled the Eucharist as a wedding feast, where the eternal Son of God enters into the most intimate union with His spouse, the Church. It is this "Communion" that makes us one with Christ, sons in the Son.

To prepare for this Communion—our New Covenant, our mystical marriage—we must, like any spouses, leave our old lives behind. As bride, we will forsake our old name for a new one. We will be forever *identified* with Another: our Beloved, Jesus Christ, the Son of God. Marriage demands that spouses make a self-sacrifice that is complete and total, as Christ's was on the cross. Yet we are weak and we are sinners, and we find the very suggestion of such sacrifice unbearable.

Here's the good news. Christ became one of us, to offer His humanity as the perfect sacrifice. In the Mass, we join our sacrifice with His, and that union makes our sacrifice perfect.

FEELING NO PAIN

The Mass is the "once for all," perfect sacrifice of Calvary, which is presented on heaven's altar for all eternity. It is not a "repeat performance." There is only one sacrifice; it is perpetual and eternal, and so it needs never be repeated. Yet the Mass is *our participation* in that one sacrifice and in the eternal life of the Trinity in heaven, where the Lamb stands eternally "as if slain."

How can this be? How can God offer sacrifice? *To whom* could God offer sacrifice?

In the Godhead, in heaven, this life-giving love goes on painlessly but eternally. The Father pours out the fullness of Himself; He holds nothing of His divinity back. He eternally fathers the Son. The Father is, above all else, a life-giving lover, and the Son is His perfect image. So what else is the Son but a life-giving lover? And He dynamically images the Father from all eternity, pouring out the life He's received from the Father; He gives that life back to the Father as a perfect expression of thanks and love. That life and love the Son received from the Father and returns to the Father *is* the Holy Spirit.

Why bring this up now? Because this is what happens in the Mass! The early Christians were so astonished by this fact that they were prone to sing about it, as in this sixth-century Syrian hymn: "Exalted are the mysteries of this temple in which the heaven and earth symbolize the most exalted Trinity and our Savior's dispensation." The Mass makes present, in time, what the Son has been doing from all eternity: loving the Father as the Father loves the Son, giving back the gift He received from the Father.

A MASSIVE CHANGE

That gift is the life we're meant to share; but before we can, we must undergo a significant change. As we are now, we're incapable of giving so much or receiving so much; the infinite fire of divine love would consume us. Yet, we cannot change on our own. That's why God gives us His own life in the sacraments. Grace makes up for the weakness of human nature. With His help, we're able to do what we couldn't do by ourselves: namely, love perfectly and sacrifice totally.

What God the Son has been doing from all eternity, He begins doing now in humanity. He doesn't change at all; for God Himself is unchanging, eternal, without beginning or end. What changes is not God but humanity.

God assumed our humanity, so that every gesture, every thought He had—from the moment He was conceived till the moment He died on the cross—everything He did on earth would be an action of the Son loving the Father. What He is from all eternity, He manifested in His humanity. Thus, perfect love now takes place in time, because God has assumed our human nature, and He has used it to express the life-giving love of the Son for the Father. Through His life and death, Jesus deified humanity. He united it to the divine.

And every time we receive the Eucharist, we receive this glorified, divinized, empowered humanity of Jesus Christ, the perfect manifestation of the divine Son's love for the Father. Only with this massive infusion of grace can we undergo the change required before we enter the life of the Trinity.

The Eucharist changes us. Now, we're able to do all the same things we'd done before—but making them divine in Christ: making our every gesture, thought, and feeling an expression of love for the Father, an action of the Son within us.

TRIBAL TROUBLES?

Marrying into any family means big changes. Marrying into the family of God means complete transformation.

What difference does it make? All the difference in the world, and then some. With this change—in the words of a fourth-century Syrian Father, Aphrahat—man becomes God's temple, as God is man's temple. We worship, as Revelation says, "in the Spirit." We dwell in the

Trinity. Now, too, we live in God's house, the Church, which is built upon rock (see Mt 7:24–27; 16:17–19). Now, we are called by His name (see Eph 4:3–6). Now, we partake of the table of the Lord (see 1 Cor 10:21). Now, we share in His flesh and blood (see Jn 6:53–56). Now, His mother is our mother (see Jn 19:26–27).

Now, we can understand why we call priests "Father" and the pope our "Holy Father"—because they are other Christs, and Christ is the perfect image of the Father. Now, we can understand why we call women religious "Sister" and "Mother"—because they are images for us of the Virgin Mary, and of Mother Church.

Now, more clearly than ever, we can understand why the saints in heaven care so much for our welfare. *We're their family!* We must never forget the Christians who have gone before us. In our prayer and our study, we must come to know their company and their help. Through the saints' example, we must learn to care as deeply for those who stand beside us during Mass each week. *Because they're our family in Christ*—and our common sainthood begins now.

Think about it: if we all persevere together, you and I will share a home forever with Christ—*with the parishioners we worship beside today.*

Does that make you feel uncomfortable? Maybe you suddenly remembered the parishioners who most get on your nerves. (I know I did.) Could heaven really be heaven if all of our neighbors are there? Could heaven be paradise if Father So-and-So makes it, too?

That's the *only* sort of heaven we should think about. Remember, we're a family of the ancient sort: a clan, a tribe. We're all in this together. That doesn't mean we'll always *feel* affection for the people we see at Mass. It does mean we must love them, bear with their weaknesses, and serve them—because they, too, have been identified with Christ. We cannot love Him without loving them. Loving difficult people will refine us. Perhaps only in heaven will our love be so perfected that we can actually *like* these people, too. St. Augustine spoke of a man who, on earth, had chronic gas problems; in heaven, his flatulence became perfect music.

BRING IT ON HOME

The communion of saints is not merely a doctrine. It is a lived reality perceived only when we live steadfast lives of faith. But it is more real than the ground we walk on. It's a permanent reality, even if its permanence is not manifested continuously in our parish.

We need, right now, to open our eyes of faith. Heaven is here. We've seen it unveiled. The communion of saints is all around us, with the angels, on Mount Zion, whenever we go to Mass.

FOUR

Rite Makes Might

THE DIFFERENCE MASS MAKES

To GO TO MASS is to go to heaven, where "God Himself . . . will wipe away every tear" (Rev 21:3–4). Yet heaven is even more than that. Heaven is where we place ourselves under judgment, where we see ourselves in the clear morning light of eternal day, and where the just Judge reads our works from the book of life. Our deeds go with us when we go to heaven. Our deeds go with us when we go to Mass.

To go to Mass is to renew our covenant with God, as at a marriage feast—for the Mass *is* the marriage supper of the Lamb. As in a marriage, we take vows, we pledge ourselves, we assume a new identity. We are changed forever.

To go to Mass is to receive the fullness of grace, the very life of the Trinity. No power in heaven or on earth can give us more than we receive in the Mass, for we receive God into ourselves.

We must never underestimate these realities. In the Mass, God has given us His very life. This is not just a metaphor, or a symbol, or a foretaste. We must go to Mass with eyes and ears, mind and heart open to *the truth* that is before us, the truth that rises like incense. God's life is a gift we must receive properly and with gratitude. He gives us grace as He has given us fire and light. Fire and light, misused, can burn us or blind us. In a similar way, grace received unworthily subjects us to judgment, and to much more dire consequences.

In every Mass, God renews His covenant with each of us, setting before us life and death, blessing and curse. We must choose the blessing for our own, and reject the curse, and we must do this from the very start.

MAKING A SPLASH

From the moment you walk into church, you place yourself under oath. By dipping your fingers into holy water, you renew the covenant begun with your baptism. Perhaps you were baptized as an infant; your parents made the decision for you. But now, with this simple motion, you make the decision for yourself. You touch the water to your forehead, your heart, your shoulders, and you sign yourself by "the name" in which you were baptized. Wrapped up in this motion is your acceptance of the creed, which your parents accepted in your name at your baptism. Wrapped up in this motion is your rejection of Satan, and all his pomps, and all his works.

Doing this, you testify, you make testimony, as you would in court. In court, a witness puts himself, his reputation, and his future on the line. If he fails to tell the truth, the whole truth, and nothing but the truth, he knows he will face severe consequences.

You, too, are under oath. Don't forget: the Latin word *sacramentum* literally means "oath." When you make the Sign of the Cross, you renew the sacrament of baptism, thus renewing your obligation to live up to the rights and duties of the New Covenant. You will love God with all your heart, and mind, and soul, and strength; you will love your neighbor as yourself.

You have especially vowed to tell the truth during this Mass. For this is the court of heaven; here, God will open the book of life; here, you will take the witness stand. Many, many times during the Mass, you will say "Amen," the Aramaic word that conveys assent and agreement: *Yes! So be it! Truly!* "Amen" is more than a response; it is a personal commitment. When you say "Amen," you commit your life, so you'd better mean it.

Thus, in the Mass, you are not merely a spectator. You are a participant. *Yours* is the covenant that you will renew. *Yours* is the covenant that Jesus Himself will renew, here and now.

OATH MEAL

Whenever God made a covenant, He also gave a program for its renewal. A covenant wasn't just a past event; it was ongoing, perpetually present, continually reactualized. Generations might pass since the covenant at Sinai; but whenever the children of Israel renewed that covenant, whenever they marked the Passover, it was as if the covenant were being made *today*.

The Mass is our perpetual renewal of the New Covenant. The Mass is a solemn oath you take before countless witnesses, as in the court of the Book of Revelation. *"And so with all the choirs of angels we sing . . ."* When heaven touches down upon earth, you receive the privilege of praying beside the angels. But you also receive the duty of living up to your prayers. Those same angels will hold you accountable for every word you pray.

And not only for what we pray, but for what we hear. Because it is God's Word that we hear proclaimed, and not the promises of some politician whom we can vote "for" or "against." We hear the Word of God, and not some news report whose reliability we may choose to doubt. In earthly courts, witnesses merely swear *on* the Bible; at Mass, we swear *to* the Bible. We hear God's Word; we will be held to it.

"I believe in one holy catholic and apostolic Church." Do we live by the teachings of that Church without stint and without exception? Studies indicate that more than 90 percent of Catholics in the United States, for example, reject the Church's teaching on artificial birth control. Yet we can assume that these same Catholics place themselves under oath each Sunday and recite the creed. What are the consequences of such enormous false witness?

"Forgive us our trespasses as we forgive those who trespass against us." We, who beg God's mercy, place this condition upon His mercy: that we will first forgive those who

have wronged us. Yet nearly all of us carry some grudges with us, even beyond the doorway of the church.

"Peace be with you. And also with you." We symbolically extend peace to every neighbor. Yet how many hours will pass between the end of the Mass and the first outburst of our temper?

"The Body of Christ. Amen." With what attention do we receive the Bread of Life, the Christ of faith and history? If we greeted an earthly king with the same attention, how would we be judged?

To hear the Word of God. To receive the Bread of Life. These are profound mysteries; they are incredible gifts; yet they are also mighty commitments. In the Mass, we receive divine life, divine power, more mighty than the greatest forces on the earth. Think about electricity, which can light your home or stop your heart. Think about fire, which can warm your family or consume a city block. These are but dim shadows of the supernatural power of God, Who created fire and formed the earth out of nothing. If we teach our children to treat electricity and fire with respect, how much more respectfully should we ourselves treat the very mysteries of heaven, which fill us in Holy Communion?

TRUTH—OR CONSEQUENCES

We cannot explain away the judgment we bring upon ourselves when we fail to live up to our witness. Hear the testimony of St. Paul: "Whoever, therefore, eats the bread or drinks the cup of the Lord in an unworthy manner will be guilty of profaning the body and blood of the Lord" (1 Cor 11:27). *Guilty of blasphemy!* This is no small matter. To ensure a pure sacrifice, the early Christians confessed their sins—in public! Today, the sacrament of confession is private, and not as burdensome. Do we make the most of it?

"This is why many of you are weak and ill, and some have died" (1 Cor 11:29). We dare not dismiss this as outdated or superstitious. Paul meant what he said, and the Church, even today, preserves this idea in its liturgy. Bad Communions bring judgment upon our heads. The priest, before receiving Communion, says: "Let it not bring me condemnation, but health in mind and body."

To receive Communion, then, is to receive heaven— or to bring the most severe punishment upon oneself. In some times and places, the weight of this judgment kept Christians away from Communion for years at a time. Yet this is not Paul's solution. Rather than stay away, he recommends repentance. "Let a man examine himself, and so eat of the bread and drink of the cup" (1 Cor 11:28).

This is an exam that no one passes. We are all sinners. No one is worthy to approach almighty God—never mind enter into Communion with Him. Even St. John, the Beloved Disciple and a model of purity and virtue, fell down in awe when he saw His best friend, Jesus Christ, in glory. How do we respond, interiorly, when the priest holds up the Host and says, "This is the Lamb of God . . ."?

No doubt about it: We must fight the spiritual battles that will win us recollection, attention, and contrition during the Mass.

TRUE LOVE ALWAYS

We want the blessing of the covenant, and not the curse. The more we are prepared for Mass, the more grace we will take away from the Mass. And remember: the grace available in the Mass is infinite—it's all the grace of heaven. The only limit is our capacity to receive it.

This blessing is pure power, though not as the world understands power. Grace means freedom, though not as the world understands freedom. Union with Christ made Simon Peter stronger than the Roman emperor Nero, even though Nero authorized Peter's death. Peter received heaven; Nero ruled the world, but was consumed by his perversions, which grew ever more depraved, driving him to suicide in the year A.D. 68.

Grace makes up for every weakness of our human nature. With God's help, we're able to do what we could never do on our own: namely, love perfectly, sacrifice completely, lay down our lives as Christ did. We will cling to nothing of the earth, preferring instead to rise to heaven.

The martyrs of the Apocalypse are the ones who speak from the altar. They are sacraments of the Eucharistic sacrifice of Christ. In their lives, they manifested the true nature of love: sacrificial self-offering.

We can live this martyrdom wherever we are. We need not travel to oppressive, anti-Christian countries to be martyrs. We need only do all the same things we've always done—but now making every one of those gestures, actions, thoughts, and feelings an expression of love for the Father, an imitation of the Son within us. That's what it means to live the Mass.

WORKING WONDERS

That's what it means to be a missionary and a martyr, restoring all things in Christ. It means cooking dinner unto Christ, and through Him to the Father, and for His children, who are yours. It means going to work and doing a job with friendship for your coworkers, and not merely to get a better wage next year, or get a promotion, but to earn an eternal inheritance.

Remember again the words of Vatican II: "[T]heir work, prayers and apostolic endeavors, their ordinary married and family life, their daily labor, their mental and physical relaxation . . . all of these become spiritual sacrifices acceptable to God through Jesus Christ. During the celebration of the Eucharist these sacrifices are most lovingly offered to the Father along with the Lord's body."

Our whole life gets caught up in the Mass and becomes our participation in the Mass. As heaven descends to earth, we lift up our earth to meet it halfway. That's the splendor of the ordinary: the workaday world becomes our Mass. That's how we bring about the Kingdom of God. When we begin to see that heaven awaits us in the Mass, we begin already to bring our home to heaven. And we begin already to bring heaven home with us.

We become martyrs, witnesses to Jesus Christ, Whose *Parousia,* Whose Presence, we know most intimately.

SUPPER'S READY

We were made as creatures on earth, but we were made for heaven, and nothing less. We were made in time like Adam and Eve, yet not to remain in an earthly paradise, but to be taken up into the eternal life of God Himself.

Now, heaven has been unveiled for us with the death and resurrection of Jesus Christ. *Now* is the Communion God has created us for. *Now*, heaven touches earth and awaits you. Jesus Christ Himself says to you: "Behold, I stand at the door and knock; if anyone hears My voice and opens the door, *I will come in to him and eat with him, and he with Me*" (Rev 3:20).

The door opens *now* on the marriage supper of the Lamb.

Sources and References

Introduction

Page 3: The statement by Pope John Paul II is taken from his Angelus Address (Nov. 3, 1996). Pope John Paul II also gave an "Address on Liturgy" to U.S. bishops during their 1998 *ad limina* visit, in which he states: "The challenge now is to . . . reach the proper point of balance, especially by entering more deeply into the contemplative dimension of worship. . . . This will happen only if we recognize that the liturgy has dimensions both local and universal, time-bound and eternal, horizontal and vertical, subjective and objective. It is precisely those tensions which give to Catholic worship its distinctive character. The universal Church is united in the one great act of praise; but it is always the worship of a particular community in a particular culture. It is the eternal worship of Heaven, but it is also steeped in time." He then concluded: "At the core of this experience of pilgrimage is our journey as sinners into the unfathomable depths of the Church's liturgy, the liturgy of creation, the liturgy of heaven, all of which are in the end the worship of Jesus Christ, the Eternal Priest, in Whom the Church and all creation are drawn into the life of the Most Holy Trinity, our true home." See Pope John Paul II, *Springtime of Evangelization* (San Diego: Basilica Press, 1999), pp. 130, 135. Pope John Paul II elucidates this vision more thoroughly in his 1995 Apostolic Letter, *Orientale Lumen* ("The Light of the East").

In Heaven Right Now

Page 11: "In the earthly liturgy . . ." *Sacrosanctum Concilium* 8.
Page 11: "Even a cursory reading . . ." Leonard L. Thompson, *The*

Book of Revelation: Apocalypse and Empire (New York: Oxford University Press, 1990), p. 53.

Given for You

Page 22: On the number of lambs sacrificed. Josephus, *Wars of the Jews* VI.9.424.

From the Beginning

Page 30: "this is the sacrifice . . ." *Didache* 14.3.

Page 31: "On the Lord's own day . . ." *Didache* 14.1.

Page 31: "As this broken bread . . ." *Didache* 9.4–5. 10.3, 10.5.

Page 33: "Structurally speaking . . ." Joseph Ratzinger, *Feast of Faith* (San Francisco: Ignatius Press, 1986), p. 57. See also pp. 51–60.

Page 33: "In the coming . . ." See Hartmut Gese, *Essays on Biblical Theology* (Minneapolis: Augsburg, 1981), pp. 128–133.

Page 34 "the place of sacrifice" See his letters to the *Ephesians* (5.2), *Trallians* (7.2), and *Philadelphians* (4) all cited in Johannes Quasten's *Patrology*, Vol. 1 (Allen, Texas: Christian Classics, 1988).

Page 34: "Take care, then . . ." St. Ignatius of Antioch, *Letters to the Philadelphians*, 4.

Page 34: "From the Eucharist and prayer . . ." St. Ignatius of Antioch, *Letter to the Smyrnaeans*, 7.

Page 34: "Let that be deemed . . ." St. Ignatius of Antioch, *Letter to the Smyrnaeans*, 8.1.

Page 34: "On the day we call . . ." St. Justin Martyr, *Apology* 1, 65–67. See also *Catechism of the Catholic Church*, no. 1345.

Page 36: "The food that has been . . ." St. Justin Martyr, *Apology* 1, 66.

Page 36: "And the offering of fine flour . . ." St. Justin Martyr, *Dialogue with Trypho*, 41.

Page 37: "Priest: The Lord be with you . . ." For a good translation of Hippolytus's liturgical text, see Lucien Deiss, *Early Sources of the Liturgy* (Staten Island, N.Y.: Alba House, 1967), pp. 29–73.

Taste and See (and Hear and Touch) the Gospel

Page 48: "You who are accustomed . . ." Origen, *On Exodus*, 13.3.

Page 50: "Dogma is by definition nothing other than . . ." Joseph

Ratzinger, "Crisis in Catechetics," *Canadian Catholic Review* (June 1983), p. 8.

Page 50: "In the dogma of the Church . . ." International Theological Commission, *On the Interpretation of Dogmas* (Origins, May 17, 1990), p. 10.

Page 55: "There is good reason . . ." Raymond Brown, S.S., *New Testament Essays* (New York: Doubleday, 1968), p. 307.

"I Turned to See"

Page 63: "a revelation should be revealing." Cited in Roland H. Bainton, *Here I Stand: A Life of Martin Luther* (New York: Mentor, 1950), p. 261.

Page 64: "The millennium is, today . . ." See Hal Lindsey, *The Late Great Planet Earth* (Grand Rapids: Zondervan, 1970).

Page 68: On the Book of Revelation as a "temple vision," see R. A. Briggs, *Jewish Temple Imagery in the Book of Revelation* (New York: Peter Lang, 1999), pp. 45–110; A. Spatofora, *From the "Temple of God" to God as the Temple: A Biblical Theological Study of the Temple in the Book of Revelation* (Rome: Gregorian University Press, 1997); J. Paulien, "The Role of the Hebrew Cultus, Sanctuary, and Temple in the Plot and Structure of the Book of Revelation," *Andrews University Seminary Studies* 33 (1995), pp. 245–64; W. Riley, "Temple Imagery and the Book of Revelation: Ancient Near Eastern Temple Ideology and Cultic Resonances in the Apocalypse," *Proceedings of the Irish Biblical Association* 6 (1982): 81–102. A majority of modern commentators (e.g., Beale, Aune, Thompson, Caird, Ladd) recognize the numerous features of John's visions as drawn from the temple liturgy (seven lampstands = the menora, the white robe as a priestly garment, etc.).

Page 70: See Joseph Ratzinger, *Eschatology* (Washington, D.C.: Catholic Univ. of America Press, 1988), p. 39 "[I]t is extremely important to note how these two aspects—the imminent destruction of Jerusalem and the Parousia—are temporarily related. . . . The fall of Jerusalem is not the end of the world but the start of a new age in salvation history" He further observes: "Nevertheless, the impression persists that the trials and tribulations entailed in the destruction of Jerusalem *are* connected in time with the events of the end of the world" (p. 40).

Who's Who in Heaven

Page 73: For a popular presentation of all four interpretive approaches to Revelation (presented side by side on every page), see S. Gregg (ed.), *Revelation: Four Views—A Parallel Commentary* (Nashville: Thomas Nelson, 1997).

Pages 77–80: On the identification of "the Woman" in Rev. 12 with the Blessed Virgin Mary (who was foreshadowed in the Old Testament by "Daughter Zion," just as she prefigures and embodies Christ's Church in the New Testament, as virgin-bride and fruitful mother), see Ignace de la Potterie, S.J., *Mary in the Mystery of the Covenant* (New York: Alba House, 1992), p. 253–63; George Montague, S.M., "Mary and the Church in the Fathers," *American Ecclesiastical Review* 123 (1950): 153; Bernard J. Le Frois, S.V.D., *The Woman Clothed with the Sun (Apoc. 12)—Individual or Collective: An Exegetical Study* (Rome: Herder, 1954); *idem*, "The Woman Clothed with the Sun," *American Ecclesiastical Review* 126 (1952): 161–80; D. J. Unger, "Did Saint John See the Virgin Mary in Glory?," *Catholic Biblical Quarterly* 11–12 (1949-50): 75–83, 155–61, 249–62, 292–300, 392–405, 405–415.

PAGE 80: "EVERYONE KNOWS THAT THIS . . ." Pope Pius X, Encyclical Letter *Ad Diem Illum Laetissimum* 24, 1904.

Page 80: On the essential reality underlying John's figurative description of the "mystery of iniquity" (e.g., "the Beasts"), see *Christian Faith and Demonology*, Congregation for the Doctrine of the Faith (Boston: Daughters of St. Paul, 1975), p. 14: "It is in effect the Book of Revelation which by revealing the enigma of the different names and symbols of Satan in Scripture, definitively unmasks his identity."

Pages 83–84: For more on the possible Solomonic background to 666 (1 Kgs 10:14), see A. Farrer. *A Rebirth of Images: The Making of St. John's Apocalypse* (London: Dacre Press, 1949), pp. 256–60. Farrer also notes: "On the sixth day of the week, and the sixth hour, says St. John, the kingdoms of Christ and Antichrist looked one another in the face in Pilate's court, and the adherents of the False Prophet (Caiaphas) firmly wrote on their foreheads the mark of the Beast, when they said, 'We have no king but Caesar'. . . . Christ's Friday victory is the supreme manifestation also of the Antichrist" (p. 259).

Apocalypse Then!

Pages 90–103: See Ignace de la Potterie, "The Apocalypse Has Already Happened," *30 Days* 9 (1995): 56–57.

Page 92: "But it is not easy . . ." *Summa Theologica* III, Supplemental Question 73; see also St. Augustine, *Epistle 80*, which St. Thomas cites.

Pages 92–94: Joseph Ratzinger, *Eschatology*, pp. 201–202: "Of its nature, the return of the Lord can be described only in images. The New Testament drew its imaginative material in this connection from Old Testament descriptions of the Day of Yahweh. . . . Other material was added by way of borrowing from the cultus . . . and the Liturgy. . . . On this basis, we can offer a faithful evaluation of the language of cosmic symbolism in the New Testament. This language is liturgical language. . . ." He continues: "This analysis allows us to draw two conclusions. The cosmic imagery of the New Testament cannot be used as a source for the description of a future chain of cosmic events. All attempts of this kind are misplaced. Instead these texts form part of a description of the mystery of the Parousia in the language of the liturgical tradition. The New Testament conceals and reveals the unspeakable coming of Christ, using language borrowed from that sphere, which is graciously enabled to express in this world the point of contact with God. *The Parousia is the highest intensification and fulfillment of the Liturgy. And the Liturgy is Parousia, a Parousia-like event taking place in our midst*" (pp. 202–203). Ratzinger adds: "*Every Eucharist is Parousia, the Lord's coming,* and yet the Eucharist is even more truly the tensed yearning that He would reveal His hidden Glory" (p. 203). He thus concludes: "Seen in this perspective, the theme of the Parousia ceases to be a speculation about the unknown. It becomes an interpretation of the Liturgy and the Christian life in their intimate connection. . . ." (p. 204) [emphasis added].

Pages 93–94: Karl Adam, *The Christ of Faith* (New York: Pantheon Books, 1957), pp. 283–84: . . . "So Catholic commentators prefer the explanation that our Lord's utterances in this speech [the Olivet Discourse] are to be interpreted as a *prophetic vision*. . . . Within this context, the fall of Jerusalem acquires primary significance in the history of salvation. For it is not the fall of any ordinary town, but the fall of the old covenant, divine judgment upon the first-born of Jahweh, because they did not know the time of their visitation. In Jesus' prophetic view, the fall of Jerusalem signifies the first act of the judgment of the world, the true introduction of the looming Last Judgment. To Jesus the town's fall was already part of the great new thing that came unawares into the world with his mission, and will reach its fulfillment in the Parousia of the Lord. And because the fall of Jerusalem, *the overture to the last judgment*, would take place within this generation, then, indeed, many of Christ's listeners would be witness to this judgment."

Page 94: On the close and profound link between the Real Presence and the Parousia, see P. Hinnebusch, "The Eucharist and the Parousia," *Homiletic and Pastoral Review* (November 1994): 15–19; G. Wainwright, *Eucharist and Eschatology* (New York: Oxford University Press, 1981); F.-X. Durrwell, *The Eucharist: Presence of Christ* (Denville, NJ: Dimension, 1974); Jean Galot, "The Theology of the Eucharistic Presence," *Review for Religious* 22 (1963: 407–26; A. J. Kenney, "Until He Comes: Eschatology and the Eucharist," *The Clergy Review* 41 (1956): 514–26.

Page 97: For a good case favoring a pre-70 A.D. date for Revelation (i.e., during the Neronian persecution, before the Jewish Revolt), see K. L. Gentry, *Before Jerusalem Fell: Dating the Book of Revelation* (Tyler, Texas: I.C.E., 1989).

Page 98: On the ancient traditions surrounding the "foundation stone" (in Hebrew, `eben shetiyah`), upon which the Jerusalem temple was built (and where the Dome of the Rock is presently located), see B. F. Meyer, "The Temple at the Navel of the Earth," in *Christus Faber: The Master-Builder of the House of God* (Pittsburgh: Pickwick Press, 1992), pp. 21–79; *idem, The Aims of Jesus* (Philadelphia: Fortress Press, 1979), pp. 185–87; Z. Vilnay, *Legends of Jerusalem* (Philadelphia: Jewish Publication Society of America, 1973), pp. 5–49; J. Jeremias, *Golgotha* (Leipzig: Pfeiffer, 1926), pp. 66–68; A. J. Wensinck, *The Idea of the Western Semites Concerning the Navel of the Earth* (Amsterdam: Johannes Muller, 1916), pp. 22–35, 54–65. For an interesting treatment of the apparent link in Revelation 20 between the "foundation stone" and "the binding of the Dragon" during "the millennium" (i.e, the Davidic covenant period from the conquest of Jerusalem in 1003 B.C. until the birth of Jesus), when the earthly Jerusalem served as a temporary prototype of the New Covenant Kingdom, see Scott Hahn, "The End: A Bible Study on the Book of Revelation" (a thirteen-tape series distributed by St. Joseph

Communication, West Covina, California; 1993); and V. Burch, *Anthropology and the Apocalypse* (London: Macmillan, 1939), pp. 139–209; E. Corsini, *The Apocalypse* (Wilmington, Delaware: Michael Glazier, 1983), pp. 361–85; and R. A. White, "Preterism and the Orthodox Doctrine of Christ's Parousia" (M.A. Thesis, Trinity Evangelical Divinity School, 1986), pp. 42–46.

Page 98: On earthly Jerusalem in A.D. 70 as the primary object of divine covenant judgment in Revelation (vs. Rome), see A. J. Beagley, *The 'Sitz Im Leben' of the Apocalypse with Particular Reference to the Role of the Church's Enemies* (New York: Walter de Gruyter, 1987); also see D. Chilton, *The Days of Vengeance: An Exposition of the Book of Revelation* (Tyler, Texas: Dominion Press, 1987).

Page 99: "Spiritually, we are Semites." Cited in J. L. McNulty in "The Bridge," *The Bridge* I (1955), p. 12.

Pages 100–102: B. F. Westcott, *The Historic Faith* (New York: Macmillan, 1890), p. 90: "The fall of Jerusalem was for the religious history of the world, an end as complete as death. The establishment of a spiritual Church was a beginning as glorious as the Resurrection."

Judgment Day

Page 108: See Augustin Cardinal Bea, "The Jewish People in the Divine Plan of Salvation," *Thought* 41 (1966): 9–32. Bea states: "[W]e must keep in mind the typical prophetic perspective in which the judgment on Jerusalem is at once the model and symbol of the Last Judgment. . . . Thus, in the well-known discourse of Jesus in Matthew 24, the historical judgment on Jerusalem and the Last Judgment so intermingle as to make it impossible to decide where the one ends and the other begins. Therefore, the judgment on Jerusalem and its destruction are part of the revelation of God to mankind; through it, in one specific episode, God displays something of that terrible reality of the judgment with which the history of mankind will be concluded. Since that reality is of decided importance for mankind, according to the Holy Scripture, it is perfectly consonant with the divine teaching to project some image of it in the history of mankind as a severe but efficacious and salutary admonishment" (pp. 22–23).

Lifting the Veil

Page 115: "We did not know . . ." See *The Orthodox Church*, Timothy Ware (Baltimore: Penguin Books, 1963), p. 269.

Page 116: "Liturgy is anticipated Parousia . . ." Joseph Ratzinger, *A New Song for the Lord* (New York: Crossroad, 1997), p. 129. He adds: "Hence, it is not the case that you think something up and then sing it; instead the song comes to you from the angels, and you have to lift up your heart so that it may be in tune with the music coming to it. Above all else, this is important: the liturgy is not a thing the monks create. It is already there before them. It is entering into the liturgy of the heavens. . . . Earthly liturgy is liturgy because and only because it joins what is already in process, the greater reality."

Page 117: P. Maniyattu, *Heaven on Earth: The Theology of Liturgical Space-time in the East Syrian Curbana* (Rome: Mar Thoma Yogam, 1995), pp. 25–26: "It is the holy eucharist which renders time eternal. Participation in the eucharistic liturgy enables one to transcend the limits of time and enter the sphere of sacred time. . . ."

Pages 118: For further development of the liturgical structure and elements of the Book of Revelation, see J.-P. Ruiz, "The Apocalypse of John and Contemporary Roman Catholic Liturgy,"; *Worship* 68 (1994): 482–504; M. M. Thompson, "Worship in the Book of Revelation," *Ex Auditu* 8 (1992): 45–54; Ugo Vanni, "Liturgical Dialogue as a Literary Form in the Book of Revelation," *New Testament Studies* 37 (1991): 348–72; B. W. Snyder, "Combat Myth in the Apocalypse: The Liturgy of the Day of the Lord and the Dedication of the Heavenly Temple" (Ph.D. Dissertation, Graduate Theological Union and Univ. of Calif., Berkeley, 1991); G. A. Gray, "The Apocalypse of Saint John the Theologian: Verbal Icon of Liturgy," (M.A. Thesis, Mount Angel Seminary, 1989); E. Cothenet, "Earthly Liturgy and Heavenly Liturgy according to the Book of Revelation," in *Roles in the Liturgical Assembly*, XII Liturgical Conference Saint-Serge (New York: Pueblo, 1981), pp. 115–35; L. Thompson, "Cult and Eschatology in the Apocalypse of John," *Journal of Religion* 49 (1969): 330–50; M. A. Shepherd, *The Paschal Liturgy and the Apocalypse* (London: Lutterworth, 1960).

Page 118: Significantly, the Catechism states: "The Book of Revelation of St. John, *read in the Church's liturgy*, first reveals to us, 'A throne stood in heaven, with one seated on the throne': 'the Lord

God.'. . ." (1137, emphasis added). This teaching of the Catechism underscores how appropriate and illuminating it is to read
and interpret the Apocalypse specifically "in the Church's liturgy,"
even as the book instructs its readers to do (Rev. 1:3); see J.-P. Ruiz
in *Ezekiel in the Apocalypse* (New York: Peter Lang, 1989), p. 488:
"[T]he liturgy was the privileged setting for understanding John's
Apocalypse. There the Scriptures were read and interpreted. . . .
Cultic vocabulary, liturgical formulae, and hymnic-doxological elements throughout the book offer evidence that this was the case."
Also see Leonard L. Thompson, *The Book of Revelation* (New York:
Oxford University Press, 1990), p. 72: "Moreover, the seer receives
his visions 'on the Lord's Day' (1:10)—*in sacro tempore*—the day of
worship in the early church, just as he expects them to be read in
the worshiping community. Prophetic revelation is both received
and proclaimed in the context of worship. Those comments by the
seer square with Paul's, who states that an 'apocalypse' makes up a
part of the service when Christians gather for worship (1 Cor.
14:26). At the end of a discussion on spiritual gifts, Paul describes a
service of worship: it includes, among other things, the singing of
hymns and the proclamation of apocalypses (1 Cor. 14:26). . . .
The prophet can use any one of several forms of worship: a prayer, a
hymn, a revelation, or even a teaching. The important thing is that
the services be orderly and controlled. The true prophet, even
when he is 'in the Spirit,' has control (1 Cor. 14:32). The close
connection between worship and apocalypse in the Book of Revelation thus conforms in several respects to what Paul says in 1 Corinthians." He concludes: "In both Revelation and the early church,
worship serves as the setting in which eschatological narratives
(such as the Book of Revelation itself) unfold. Furthermore, in both
Revelation and the churches of Asia Minor, worship realizes the
kingship of God and his just judgment; through liturgical celebration eschatological expectations are experienced presently. Hymns,
thanksgivings, doxologies, and acclamations realize in the context
of worship the eschatological message. . . . The Book of Revelation, by functioning in communal worship of Asia Minor as heavenly
worship functions in the book itself, links heaven and earth. The
work mediates its own message" (pp. 72–73). Also see David E.
Aune, *The Cultic Setting of Realized Eschatology in Early Christianity* (Lei-
den: E. J. Brill, 1972).
Page 121: "first confess your transactions . . ." *Didache* 14.13